Cases and Active Learning Exercises in Managerial Accounting

L-21214-5

Cases and Active Learning Exercises in Managerial Accounting

ALAN J. RICHARDSON, EDITOR
YORK UNIVERSITY

THOMSON

NELSON

Australia   Canada   Mexico   Singapore   Spain   United Kingdom   United States

THOMSON

NELSON

Cases and Active Learning Exercises in Managerial Accounting
by Alan J. Richardson

Associate Vice President, Editorial Director:
Evelyn Veitch

Publisher:
Rod Banister

Marketing Manager:
Kathaleen McCormick

Developmental Editor:
Jim Polley

Permissions Coordinator:
Sheila Hall

Copy Editor/Proofreader:
Matthew Kudelka

Manufacturing Coordinator:
Joanne McNeil

Design Director:
Ken Phipps

Interior Design:
Tammy Gay

Cover Design:
Johanna Liburd

Compositor:
ICC Macmillan Inc.

Printer:
Thomson West

Library and Archives Canada Cataloguing in Publication Data

Richardson, Alan J. (Alan John), 1955—Cases and active learning exercises in managerial accounting / Alan J. Richardson.

Includes bibliographical references. ISBN 978-0-17-644128-9

1. Managerial accounting—Case studies. 2. Managerial accounting— Problems, exercises, etc. I. Title.

HF5657.4.R53 2007   658.15'11
C2007-900668-X

Copyright Acknowledgment

Page 12: Reprinted by permission from Case Research Journal. Copyright 1993 Lunberg, C.C. and Enz, C. and the North American Case Research Association. All rights reserved.

CONTENTS

TABLE OF FIGURES

PREFACE

This book is a companion to *Cases in Financial Accounting: A Principles-Based Approach* (Alan J. Richardson, ed., Thomson Nelson, 2007). Both texts share the same philosophy that effective accounting education requires students to appreciate the inherent flexibility of accounting information and hence the need to develop and/or use information that fits the decision for which it is intended. Whether you are a user or a preparer of accounting information, this perspective will help you avoid the personal, business, and societal problems that arise from an uncritical use of accounting information.

We believe that this philosophy must be reflected in all accounting courses. It is irresponsible to pretend in introductory courses that accounting information unproblematically reflects economic reality only to demonstrate in advanced courses that the choice of accounting policies can dramatically change the reality that is presented to decision makers. This concern applies to corporate stakeholders, who base their assessment of an organization on its financial statements, as well as to the organization's managers, who use internal data to make operating decisions and to reward performance. The materials presented in this text are intended to allow instructors to introduce students to the richness and complexity of accounting information from their first course in accounting and through their entire program.

FEATURES OF THIS TEXT

This text focuses on those areas of management accounting where the choices of accounting policies have the greatest impact on operating decisions: short-term capacity use, cost allocation (particularly as this affects product mix and pricing decisions), transfer pricing, performance evaluation (including budget-based control systems and variance analysis), compensation decisions, and negotiations with other participants in the value chain.

The text uses two distinct approaches to provide students with a rich understanding of management accounting issues. In the first part of the book we provide a series of short cases — typically no more than a few pages — that can be used to supplement traditional lecture courses or as assignments and examinations. These cases require students to use traditional and contemporary accounting techniques to analyze decision problems and make recommendations. The use of case analysis and discussion is intended to develop students' professional and business analysis skills and to provide them with experience in the following:

- Identifying relevant information in complex circumstances.
- Applying analytical models to diagnose and understand causes and consequences.
- Communicating analyses and conclusions to others.
- Developing group skills, including an appreciation for alternative points of view.
- Problem solving and generating realistic alternative courses of action.

- Decision making, and the application of criteria in making choices.
- Justifying recommendations based on evidence and logic.

In the second part of the book, we provide a series of active learning exercises to illustrate how management accounting information is assembled through interactions among people in the organization, and to allow students to see how this information is used in negotiations both within and beyond the organization. Again, these exercises are short, require little set-up or administrative effort, and can be used to introduce or reinforce the learning objectives for a particular class.

These exercises will allow students to develop an appreciation for the range of contexts in which management accounting information arises and for the creative ways in which this information can be used in negotiations. The text provides a brief introduction to negotiation theory to help students recognize the types of negotiations they will be facing and the strategies for information use that will arise in different contexts. These exercises deal with such issues as negotiations with customers and suppliers, interviews for generating activity-based cost information, negotiations among managers over the choice of performance evaluation criteria, and the use of management accounting information in corporate restructuring.

All of the materials presented in this text have been tested as in-class exercises, as assignments, or as examination materials. We are grateful to our students at the Queen's School of Business, Queen's University, and the Schulich School of Business, York University, for encouraging us to develop innovative classroom materials to ensure that they will be well prepared for their future careers. We are also grateful to Teresa Colavecchia, Filomena Petrilli, and Mary Rizzo at the Schulich School of Business for providing superb administrative support for our courses and projects such as this book.

CONTRIBUTING AUTHORS

Tony Dimnik, Ph.D., teaches accounting at the Queen's School of Business and is a speaker on many executive programs. His current research is on Open Book Management, the portrayal of accountants in cinema, and the role of management accountants in organizations. He has been audit committee chair of several companies and is the former director of the Queen's Executive MBA Program. After obtaining a diploma in radio arts from Lethbridge Community College, he worked in the media for ten years before returning for a B.Admin. at the University of Regina and a Ph.D. in accounting at the Ivey School of Business (University of Western Ontario, 1988).

Prem M. Lobo, BBA, CA, CBV, CPA, is an instructor in the accounting area of the Schulich School of Business and is a Senior Associate with Rosen & Associates, where he specializes in business valuations, damages quantification, and forensic accounting. He holds a BBA (with distinction) from the Schulich School of Business and is a chartered accountant, chartered business valuator, and certified public accountant. He is the author of two study guides in accounting, a contributing author to *Cases in Financial Accounting* (Alan Richardson, ed.), and a contributing editor to *Understanding Financial Analysis in Litigation* by Errol Soriano. He publishes actively in a variety of journals and periodicals, including *Lawyer's Weekly* and *CA Magazine*.

Charles Plant, MBA, CA (Schulich School of Business, York University), is a Managing Director at Q1 Capital Partners, an investment bank that specializes in raising capital, and in mergers and acquisitions, for firms in the technology, industrial product, and consumer product sectors. Over the past 25 years, Charles has worked with more than 50 emerging businesses as a founder, CEO, CFO, banker, accountant, or senior adviser. He served as President and CEO of Synamics Inc., a telecommunications applications software developer, and as President and CEO of Speech Dynamics, a call centre systems integrator. Charles currently lectures in Management Accounting at York University's Schulich School of Business.

Alan J. Richardson, Ph.D., FCGA, is Professor and Chair of the Accounting Area, Schulich School of Business. He teaches management accounting and control in the Schulich MBA program and the Kellogg-Schulich EMBA program. He was founding editor of the CAAA journal *Accounting Perspectives* and sits on the editorial boards of ten academic journals. He has published in a variety of academic and professional journals, including *Accounting Organizations and Society, Contemporary Accounting Research, Journal of Accounting Research*, and *Accounting Historians Journal*. He is also the editor of *Cases in Financial Accounting: A Principles-Based Approach* (Thomson Nelson 2007).

C H A P T E R   1

CASES AND ACTIVE LEARNING IN MANAGEMENT ACCOUNTING

> Management accounting is a system of measuring and providing operational and financial information that guides managerial action, motivates behaviors, and supports and creates the cultural values necessary to achieve an organization's strategic objectives.[1]

The management accounting system provides the key information used to run organizations.[2] It serves as a common language by which people within an organization can communicate with one another about the efficiency and effectiveness of organizational operations. Management accounting also provides measures of the key management models through which we implement organizational strategies. It is impossible, for example, to implement "lean production"[3] or "value-based management"[4] without measures of cost and performance generated by the management accounting system. Management accounting provides a set of information that helps us understand how to achieve organizational objectives and that provides feedback on how well we are doing.

More than this, however, management accounting is a profession dedicated to applying financial and strategic knowledge to organizational problems. While all managers must have a working knowledge of management accounting and its role in operational decision making, the professional management accountant will have the knowledge and skills to ensure that senior management has access to, and the ability to use, management accounting information to implement organizational strategies.

---

[1] J. Bell, S. Ansari, T. Klammer, and C. Lawrence, *Strategy and Management Accounting* V1.2 (Boston: Houghton Mifflin), p. 4. http://college.hmco.com/accounting/ansari/management/1e/students/modules/mod11.pdf.

[2] The generic term "organization" (rather than firm or business) is used to reflect the fact that management accounting has a role in the private and public sectors, and in profit and non-profit sectors.

[3] "Lean production" was pioneered at Toyota and involves the use of just-in-time production methods, cellular manufacturing techniques, and continuous improvement.

[4] "Value-based management" is a philosophy of management that links all performance measurement and operations to maximizing shareholder value.

Management accounting is thus both a body of knowledge and a set of professional skills.

In choosing this book as part of your course, your instructor has made a commitment to help you develop a rich set of management accounting skills that will allow you to be an effective manager, consultant, or professional management accountant. This book is intended as a supplement to your management accounting textbook and lectures. It is a tool with which you will be able to sharpen both your understanding of management accounting and your ability to more effectively use management accounting information.

Consider the taxonomy summarized in Figure 1.1. Bloom (1956) developed this taxonomy to reflect changes in an individual's cognitive skills as he or she gains mastery of a field. The hierarchy begins with simple factual knowledge, and then continues through comprehension and application to the higher-order skills of analysis, synthesis, and evaluation. To be a skilled practitioner of any profession, you will have to have mastered all six levels of this hierarchy. The question is this: Where in your program of studies do you start to develop these skills? We contend that you must start from your first exposure to a subject.

In most introductory university courses and introductory textbooks, the focus is on the first three levels of this hierarchy. The intent is to ensure that you know the key vocabulary in the field, the meaning of each term, and how to use these concepts to solve problems. For example, if you have knowledge of cost allocation procedures and comprehend the meaning of terms such "allocation base," "cost object," and "activity level," then you should be able to apply this knowledge when provided with the total costs to be allocated and the proportion of the allocation base represented by a particular cost object. This level of knowledge, however, will not tell you whether you have chosen the correct allocation base, or whether the cost should be allocated to the cost object at all in a particular decision situation. These types of questions require the higher-level skills. You must be able to analyze the decision to be made, generate creative alternatives, and evaluate the consequences of implementing your alternatives.

We believe that students can and should be exposed to these higher-level skills throughout their university careers. From your first course in accounting, you should recognize that accounting information is flexible and that management must make choices to ensure that the information suits the use that will be made of the information.[5] It is also important for users of this information to recognize the flexibility of accounting information so that they can properly assess whether the information provided is suitable for their needs. Both the producers and the users of accounting information need to be able to analyze the information, synthesize information from multiple sources, and evaluate the quality of the information received. The cases and simulations in this book are intended to allow you to practise these skills.

---

[5] A companion text in financial accounting is also based on this premise. See A.J. Richardson, ed., *Cases in Financial Accounting: A Principles-Based Approach* (Scarborough, ON: Thomson Nelson, 2007).

FIGURE 1.1: Bloom's Taxonomy of Learning Objectives

Competence	Skills Demonstrated
Knowledge	observation and recall of information; knowledge of dates, events, places; knowledge of major ideas; mastery of subject matter
	Question Cues: list, define, tell, describe, identify, show, label, collect, examine, tabulate, quote, name, who, when, where, etc.
Comprehension	understanding information; grasp meaning; translate knowledge into new context; interpret facts, compare, contrast, order, group, infer causes, predict consequences
	Question Cues: summarize, describe, interpret, contrast, predict, associate, distinguish, estimate, differentiate, discuss, extend
Application	use information; use methods, concepts, theories in new situations; solve problems using required skills or knowledge
	Questions Cues: apply, demonstrate, calculate, complete, illustrate, show, solve, examine, modify, relate, change, classify, experiment, discover
Analysis	seeing patterns; organization of parts; recognition of hidden meanings; identification of components
	Question Cues: analyze, separate, order, explain, connect, classify, arrange, divide, compare, select, explain, infer
Synthesis	use old ideas to create new ones; generalize from given facts; relate knowledge from several areas; predict, draw conclusions
	Question Cues: combine, integrate, modify, rearrange, substitute, plan, create, design, invent, what if?, compose, formulate, prepare, generalize, rewrite
Evaluation	compare and discriminate between ideas; assess value of theories, presentations; make choices based on reasoned argument; verify value of evidence; recognize subjectivity
	Question Cues: assess, decide, rank, grade, test, measure, recommend, convince, select, judge, explain, discriminate, support, conclude, compare, summarize

Source: From Benjamin S. Bloom et al., Taxonomy of Educational Objectives Book 1. Published by Allyn & Bacon, Boston, MA. Copyright © 1984. Reprinted by permission of the publishers.

Beyond the *cognitive skills* reflected in Bloom's taxonomy, management accounting represents a set of *professional skills* that are necessary in order to successfully implement the organization's strategy. CMA Canada refers to these as "enabling competencies"[6] and summarizes them in four categories:

- Problem Solving and Decision Making
- Leadership and Group Dynamics
- Professionalism and Ethical Behaviour
- Communication

Case analysis allows you to practise your problem-solving and decision-making skills (including ethical decision-making skills, which may be summarized as exercising competence with integrity; see Figure 1.2). It also allows you to practise your communication skills, especially your written communications. If the case analysis is assigned as a group exercise, you will also have opportunities to practise your leadership and group dynamics skills (at least behind closed doors!). The active learning exercises in this book provide additional opportunities for you to practise problem-solving and decision-making skills, and leadership and group dynamics skills, in a context relevant to management accounting. Management accounting information is used as part of the day-to-day routines of organizations. It is an important part of interacting with colleagues, customers, and suppliers. The active learning exercises provide insights into these interactions.

Real business decisions are rarely well defined. Managers must make decisions every day when faced with uncertainties and a number of reasonable alternatives. The mark of an exceptional manager is how well he or she handles these types of decisions. The "case method," as pioneered by the Harvard Business School and now used in many business schools around the world, was developed to provide students with opportunities to practise these skills in the classroom. This style of case was modelled on the "clinical rounds" used in medical education (where students accompany an experienced practitioner and examine real patients) and the "moot courts" used in legal education (where students take on the role of judge, prosecutor, or defender and reargue classic legal cases). A good case discussion at a business school should allow you to practise the diagnostic skills of a clinician and the rhetorical skills of a lawyer.

The cases in this book are based on Harvard's philosophy, but with a difference. The typical Harvard case is anywhere from 10 to 90 pages long and is meant to provide a rich and challenging setting where experienced managers can refine their decision-making skills. Harvard cases are designed for graduate education; they are intended for experienced managers who have returned to school to improve their management skills. In order to analyze these cases, you need some background knowledge and the basic skills of a practising manager. Each case requires hours of preparation followed by a full class for discussion.

---

[6] For the CMA competency map, see http://www.cma-canada.org/multimedia/CMA_Canada/Document_Library/Attachments/CompetencyMap05.pdf.

FIGURE 1.2: Ethical Decision Making (Exercising Competence with Integrity)

The following extracts from professional codes of ethics reinforce the need to combine technical competence in management accounting with sound ethical decision making.

CGA Ontario Code of Ethical Principals

A professional organization and its members are granted the legal right by society to organize itself, to control entrance into the profession and to formulate standards of behaviour governing its members. In return for this right, CGA Ontario's members of the profession are to act in the interest of society and its members. Provincial and federal Acts, and Code of Ethical Principles and Rules of Conduct, formalize this arrangement. In order to fulfil this responsibility, professionals must have a number of important character traits, as well as the skill to make expert technical and moral judgments that serve the interests of society. (CGA Code of Ethical Principals[*])

CMA Code of Professional Ethics:

Ethical Professionals should be governed by two basic concepts:

1. They must be competent—this means;
   a. they must know the Body of Knowledge in their area of practice, and
   b. they must have the technical skill to apply their knowledge
2. they must have integrity — this means;
   a. they must have a keen sense of responsibility to their client or employer and to the public, and
   b. they must retain that sense of independence that will enable them to exercise their professional judgment without restriction or bias. (CMA Code of Professional Ethics[**])

CA Quebec Code of Professional Ethics:

- Whether his[/her] duties and obligations be towards the public, a client or an employer, a member shall, in all circumstances before entering into a contract relating to the practice of the profession, consider the extent of his[/her] proficiency, knowledge and the means at his[/her] disposal. He[/she] shall not, in particular, undertake work for which he[/she] is not sufficiently prepared or for which he[/she] does not have the proficiency or knowledge required without obtaining the necessary assistance.
- A member shall abstain from practising in conditions likely to impair the quality of his[/her] services and the dignity of the profession.
- A member shall abstain from intervening in the personal affairs of his[/her] client or employer on matters outside the scope of his[/her] contract.
- A member shall act with due care, in keeping with current professional accounting and assurance standards, with the other standards, rules, and guidance and guidelines set out in the Canadian Institute of Chartered Accountants Handbook and with current scientific knowledge. (CA Code of Ethics[***])

---

[*] This extract is from http://www.cga-ontario.org/contentfiles/publications_promotions/ethic.aspx. Please refer to the original text for further details.

[**] This extract is from http://www.cma-canada.org/saskatchewan/members/codeofethicsjuly2002.pdf. Please refer to the original text for further details.

[***] This extract is from http://ocaq.qc.ca/pdf/ang/2_protection/2_3_deontologie.pdf. Please refer to the original test for further details.

The cases in this book are designed to provide an entry into the analysis of more complex materials. Each case is short — typically only a few pages long. Though most contain multiple issues, they are not as complex as the Harvard-style full teaching cases. The cases in this book can be read quickly and allow you to practise your skills in simpler settings. Most of the cases are based on situations encountered in practice; however, the essence of the problem has been extracted to provide a focused context in which you can practise your analytic skills. They are designed so that you can use them as a supplement to lectures in order to test your technical knowledge in a decision-making context. You will be able to identify alternatives, consider their consequences, and make recommendations. As you work your way through the cases in this book, your abilities and your confidence in handling more complex problems will increase.

You may already have been exposed to business simulations (business games) in which you compete against others in teams by deciding on the inputs to a computer model of business behaviour. These simulations allow you to experiment with all aspects of a business model (e.g., marketing, research and development, production technologies) but rarely allow you to directly negotiate the outcomes with others. The active learning exercises in this book are also unique in focusing on short, intensive face-to-face negotiations. We believe that you will learn about management accounting concepts through the use of these exercises; but perhaps more importantly, you will gain some hands-on experience with the creative ways in which people can use this information beyond the constraints imposed by the needs of computer inputs.

Our development of the cases and active learning exercises in this book is based on the emerging role of management accounting as a key aspect of strategy implementation in organizations. This role deserves a brief comment before you begin your work.

STRATEGIC THINKING IN MANAGEMENT ACCOUNTING

One of the major changes in management accounting practice over the past 20 years has involved a redefinition of the role of the management accountant from that of a provider of information to assist management decision making to that of a strategic adviser and member of the senior management team. In 1999 the U.S. Institute of Management Accountants released a report titled "Counting More, Counting Less"[7] that captured the essence of the changing role of management accountants. The new management accountant is less concerned with the numbers themselves and more concerned with generating value based on a sophisticated and strategic use of both qualitative and quantitative information.

The new role of the management accountant is now reflected in the definitions of management accounting used by professional bodies (e.g., see the definition of management accounting used by the U.S. Institute of Management Accountants in

---

[7] Institute of Management Accountants, *Counting More, Counting Less: Transformation of the Management Accounting Profession* (Montvale, NJ: IMA, 1999).

FIGURE 1.3: Institute of Management Accountants, USA

Management Accounting:

- is the internal business-building role of accounting and finance professionals who design, implement, and manage internal systems that support effective decisions; support, plan, and control the organization's value-creating operations. Management accounting and finance professionals directly support an organization's strategic goals.
- is about building value inside organizations. Value is built by focusing on economic analysis of productive processes, sales, and customer profitability, and the value of employees and assets, both tangible and intangible.
- is focused on operations and the value chain, the leading indicators and harbingers of financial results, as opposed to the historical activities of external financial reporting and auditing. It is by nature forward looking and focused on seeking opportunities for growth and improvement.
- focuses on the real internal economics of the enterprise — creating new business, optimizing existing business processes, and analyzing customer value — that create long-term, sustainable value.

Source: Institute of Management Accountants, Montvale, New Jersey, USA. Adapted with permission.

Figure 1.3) and in descriptions of what management accountants do (e.g., see the description of the role of a CMA by CMA Canada in Figure 1.4).

The strategic role of management accountants has been supported by the development of new costing techniques such as activity-based costing, by new frameworks for identifying value-creating and value-destroying operations such as activity-based management, and by performance measurement systems linked to strategy such as the balanced scorecard. These new techniques, coupled with traditional costing and performance measurement systems, provide the management accountant with a strong base of financial management skills from which to contribute to the strategic development of the organization.

Besides technical skills in accounting, the new role of the management accountant requires the skills of a management consultant and change agent. A management consultant must determine, in consultation with the client, the most appropriate role to take in dealing with an assignment. This role may include leading, facilitating, mentoring, or coaching.[8] In a leadership role, the management accountant will identify the strategic objective to be implemented, assemble the appropriate resources, and monitor and motivate performance. As a facilitator, the management accountant will ensure that group processes within the senior management team are effective — specifically, that the team gathers the right information, identifies issues, prioritizes issues, generates and evaluates

---

[8] These potential roles are taken from the Common Body of Knowledge of the International Council of Management Consulting Institutes (see http://www.icmci.org/AboutUs/2002%20CBK%20ICMCI%20version.doc).

FIGURE 1.4: Certified Management Accountants — Canada

Certified Management Accountants (CMAs) do more than just measure value — they create it. As the leaders in management accounting, CMAs actively apply a unique mix of financial expertise, strategic insight, innovative thinking and a collaborative approach to help grow successful businesses.

Working in organizations of all sizes and types, CMAs provide an integrating perspective to business decision-making, applying best management practices in strategic planning, finance, operations, sales and marketing, information technology, and human resources to identify new market opportunities, ensure corporate accountability, and help organizations maintain a long-term competitive advantage.

CMAs have unique competencies in cost management, strategic performance measurement, process management, risk management and assurance services, and stakeholder reporting, coupled with the ability to connect strategy with operations and anticipate customer and supplier needs. They have a holistic view of business, able to identify issues, envision and chart solutions, and engage the appropriate measures and people within the organization to achieve the desired results. CMAs are considered both leaders and solid team players, which translates into a unique and effective style of management.

Unlike other accounting and business professionals, who specialize in financial reporting, auditing, theoretical applications or after-the-fact verification, the CMA is equipped to look to the future to provide real-world strategic direction, business management and leadership.

Source: Reprinted with permission of Certified Management Accountants of Canada.

a set of reasonable alternatives, and reaches a consensus recommendation (see Chapter 2 for further details). As a mentor, the management accountant will help others in the senior management team develop the skills necessary to succeed in their roles. Finally, as a coach, the management accountant will encourage the senior management team to achieve its potential and, in particular, will ensure that management accounting information is being used with due regard to its strengths and limitations.

When the management accountant acts as a leader, typically he or she will also be acting as a change agent to move the organization to a higher level of performance. Change is often seen as threatening in organizations since the status quo is psychologically comfortable to employees and may be supported by many social arrangements and incentives. In order to bring about change, the management accountant must be able to:

- provide a vision that demonstrates the need for change and clearly shows what changes are necessary;
- bring together a team to implement change that works effectively together and that possesses the right skills to accomplish the desired end;
- communicate effectively in order to build enthusiasm and commitment;

- negotiate effectively both within the organization and with key stakeholders; *and*
- maintain a broader perspective to see how the change affects the long-run performance of the organization.[9]

The skills required of management accountants are complex and involve an ability to deal effectively with others. While the financial accountant produces financial statements that may be used by anonymous external users, the management accountant is usually involved with the people and decisions that require management accounting information. This book is intended to help you develop these skills through two distinct approaches. In the first part of the book we present a series of management accounting cases that allow you to practise the technical and analytical skills needed to reach sound business decisions. In the second part we present a series of active learning exercises designed to allow you to interact with others in order to better understand how management accounting information is generated through interactions with others and used in negotiations and other interactions. In Chapter 6 we discuss the skills you will need to apply your newly gained knowledge successfully.

This book will provide you with opportunities to practise a key set of competencies that are now seen as essential for managers, consultants, and accountants. By working through the cases, you will develop the ability to interpret complex information, to apply strategic and critical thinking skills, and to communicate effectively with peers and clients. By working through the active learning exercises, you will develop an appreciation for the ways in which context affects the use of management accounting information and how that information can support strategic interactions with others both inside and outside the organization. These skills and perspectives on management accounting will help you be a more effective practitioner.

---

[9] D. Buchanan and D. Boddy, *The Expertise of the Change Agent: Public Performance and Backstage Activity* (Englewood Cliffs, NJ: Prentice-Hall, 1992).

C H A P T E R   2

A GUIDE TO CASE ANALYSIS

Most students find case analysis frustrating and difficult. It is frustrating because a case does not provide prepackaged information that neatly fits the requirements of the analytical tools of accounting. A case will include the information that is essential to consider in coming to a recommendation, but it may also include information that is tangential or even misleading. Sometimes the information you need is not included in the case but is implied by the circumstances. For example, the industry in which a firm operates provides important clues about the business environment and the constraints under which the firm operates. One of the important skills to develop is the ability to identify the information and assumptions that are crucial to your analysis.

Students find case analysis difficult because there is no one correct answer. Case analysis is not about applying fixed techniques to arrive at a number or at some other single solution. The lack of a single correct answer, however, does not mean there are not better and worse answers. In part, the quality of a case analysis is related to the process you follow and to how you communicate this process. A good case analysis will provide evidence that you have applied sound diagnostic skills to the correct information, considered a reasonable set of alternatives, and made a reasoned recommendation. Two people may analyze the same case and come to completely opposite recommendations, yet each could be recognized as having done good work. The purpose of this brief guide is to help you to understand the case analysis process and to write better case analyses.

There are many guides to case analysis to which you can refer. Figure 2.1 provides two alternatives to which you can compare the approach described below. Each of these approaches tends to cover the same ground and will help you develop a sound analysis. Like case analysis itself, the use of any guide to case analysis requires practice and good judgment. *Do not apply the guide in a mechanical or checklist manner. Think about what each step is asking you to do, and why. Each step contributes toward making a reasoned recommendation based on consideration of a range of alternatives.*

FIGURE 2.1: Examples of Alternative Approaches to Case Analysis

From C.C. Lundberg and C. Enz (1993), "A Framework for Student Case Preparation," *Case Research Journal* 13 (Summer): 144.

- Step 1: Gaining Familiarity
  a. In general — determine who, what, how, where, and when (the critical facts in a case).
  b. In detail — identify the places, persons, activities, and contexts of the situation.
  c. Recognize the degree of certainty/uncertainty of acquired information.

- Step 2: Recognizing Symptoms
  a. List all indicators (including stated "problems") that something is not as expected or as desired.
  b. Ensure that symptoms are not assumed to be the problem (symptoms should lead to identification of the problem).

- Step 3: Identifying Goals
  a. Identify critical statements by major parties (e.g., people, groups, the work unit, etc.).
  b. List all goals of the major parties that exist or can be reasonably inferred.

- Step 4: Conducting the Analysis
  a. Decide which ideas, models, and theories seem useful.
  b. Apply these conceptual tools to the situation.
  c. As new information is revealed, cycle back to sub-steps a and b.

- Step 5: Making the Diagnosis
  a. Identify predicaments (goal inconsistencies).
  b. Identify problems (discrepancies between goals and performance).
  c. Prioritize predicaments/problems regarding timing, importance, etc.

- Step 6: Doing the Action Planning
  a. Specify and prioritize the criteria used to choose action alternatives.
  b. Discover or invent feasible action alternatives.
  c. Examine the probable consequences of action alternatives.
  d. Select a course of action.
  e. Design an implementation plan/schedule.
  f. Create a plan for assessing the action to be implemented.

From R. Stillman (ed.), *Public Administration: Concepts and Cases*, 8th ed. (Boston: Houghton Mifflin, 2005):

- Become familiar with case substance — facts, info, availability
- Determine central issues — decisions to be made, who is responsible, what are issues
- Identify objectives and goals to be achieved — what is possible, desirable
- Ascertain resources and constraints — what resources are available, what are obstacles, who supports and opposes
- Ascertain the nature of the conflict — what is the substance of the conflict, can the issues be resolved
- Identify dynamics of behavior — who is leading, are there interpersonal conflicts, are stakeholders making effective arguments

- Determine major alternatives — what hasn't been considered, are alternatives complementary or mutually exclusive
- Assess consequences of likely decisions and actions — what actions are likely to result from decisions made, what are the unintended consequences
- Consider appropriate strategies and priorities — what are the most effective ways of achieving and implementing objectives and decisions, and are there intermediate stages/steps

To help you think about case analysis, we have broken down the process into the following stages:

- information gathering;
- issue identification;
- issue prioritization;
- alternative generation;
- recommendation; *and*
- implementation issues.

The case analysis process is summarized in Figure 2.2. We will elaborate on each of these stages below.

FIGURE 2.2: The Case Analysis Process

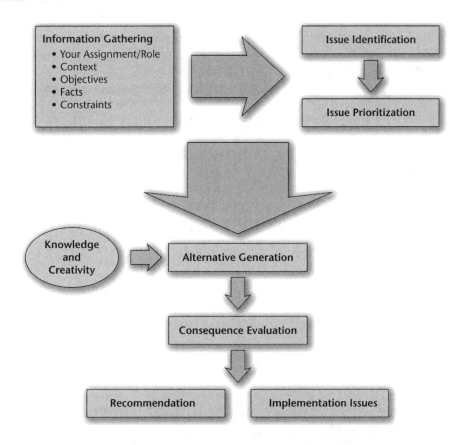

INFORMATION GATHERING

The first stage in any case analysis is straightforward: read the case. In fact, you may need to read the case several times. In the rest of this guide you will learn what to look for as you read. In brief, you are reading to understand your role in completing the case analysis and to identify the key facts, the issues, the users of the information and their objectives, and any factors that may limit the range of alternatives that can be considered. Rosen[1] summarized what to look for as you read a case as the following mantra: *facts, objectives, constraints*.

(A) UNDERSTAND YOUR ASSIGNMENT

One of the most important parts of the case to understand is the "required" assignment. Most case analyses specifically ask you to prepare your analysis from the perspective of a particular role communicating to a particular person using a particular format. This is typically found in the final sentence or paragraph of the case. For example, you may be asked to assume the role of a staff accountant preparing a memo for the senior management of a company considering a change in product mix, or you may be asked to provide a report from the perspective of an owner/manager negotiating a contract with a supplier. The "required" part of the case is important because it provides the terms of reference for your assignment and, most importantly, identifies the "client" you are serving.

(B) UNDERSTAND THE CONTEXT

As part of your first reading of the case, identify any aspects of the business and its environment that may affect the operational decisions facing the firm. For example, identify the industry in which the company operates and the technology the firm uses to produce its goods and services. Determine whether the company is in good financial condition or in crisis. Identify the decisions to be made. Identify management's motives and incentives, and try to assess whether the information that management is working with is reliable. (In large companies this may be a question of the quality of the internal control system — that is, the steps management has taken to ensure the reliability of the information on which it bases its decisions; in smaller companies it may simply be a question of the competence of the manager making the key assumptions required by the management accounting system.)

Discussing the case with others may help you identify important contextual factors. Based on our personal experiences, exposure to different businesses, and our own reading of the business press, each of us develops a store of tacit knowledge about how the world works. When you discuss cases in groups, you become aware that you have tacit knowledge that you can use to educate your peers and enrich your own

---

[1] L.S. Rosen, *Financial Accounting: A Canadian Casebook* (Toronto: Prentice-Hall, 1982).

analyses of cases. Don't be afraid to use this knowledge in your analyses; however, you may want to verify that what you "know" is valid. Your understanding of the context of business will also improve as you take more courses in your educational program. You may not be able to identify all of the important contextual variables initially, but with practice your skill at this will improve.

(C) IDENTIFY *IMPORTANT* CASE FACTS

Too often, students when analyzing a case waste their time (and the time of the person reading the analysis) by repeating the facts of the case. Your analysis need only mention those facts which are relevant. Imagine that you and a friend are crossing a road and that your friend is about to step off the curb in front of a car. What do you call out? Most likely you yell something short and forceful that will trigger the response that will save your friend's life, like "Car!" You probably don't yell: "Look! A black two-door late model sedan!" The key fact in this situation is the existence of the car because of the danger it poses to your friend's life. If on the other hand you and your friend were on a car dealer's lot looking for a particular type of car to buy, calling out the colour and style of the car would be relevant to the decision being made.

Any time case facts are mentioned in your case write-up, they should move your analysis forward. The important facts are the ones that help you identify issues and evaluate alternatives. Do not simply repeat case facts in your analysis — tell the reader why those facts are important to your analysis. If you have restated a case fact, ask yourself: "Why is this piece of information important to me? How does it affect my thinking about business decisions in this company?" The most effective way to identify which case facts are important is to have a model or framework to guide your analysis.

Part of your instructor's role is to provide you with these frameworks, which you will practise using by applying them to the cases in this book. These frameworks may include tools for quantitative analysis. For example, the case might concern short-term cash flow problems. One way to identify such issues is to develop a cash budget. The purpose of such frameworks is to help you identify — and in some cases create through calculations — the key data on which to base your analysis.

ISSUE IDENTIFICATION

Most cases focus on a particular issue or set of issues. When reading the case, keep a list of all of the issues you come across. In a management decision context, issues are any choices management must make regarding how to allocate resources, coordinate action, or evaluate and reward performance. Those choices will have a material impact on the welfare of the firm.

It is important to use your own judgment when reading the issues identified by the characters in the case. It is not uncommon for people engulfed in problems to be unable to see the key issues clearly; your role is to provide an objective overview of the case.

ISSUE PRIORITIZATION

You will probably encounter multiple issues in the case. Not all issues are equally important. It may not be crucial for you to spend a lot of time on some of the issues. The key is to prioritize them — that is, list them in order of importance. The importance of various issues depends on the objectives of the decision maker in the case and the consequences of the issues. Obviously, any issue that could affect the survival of the firm is central. An issue that is short-term and is likely to resolve itself is probably not worth acting on.

Be careful also to differentiate between symptoms and root causes. To diagnose issues successfully, you must be able to look beyond the symptoms to see what is causing the problem. For example, a company may be experiencing cash shortages and high turnover. A consultant who suggests a bank loan and employee recognition awards, but who misses the company's too rapid expansion and overworked key personnel, will not be helping the firm survive. The case may suggest that a key issue is how to measure costs, but on analysis you may conclude that the company is not providing the right incentives to employees, or you may conclude that the action proposed is inconsistent with the company's strategy. Before trying to provide a solution, be sure you understand the issue(s).

ALTERNATIVE GENERATION

Once the issues have been identified, you must develop a plan of action. There will be multiple ways of handling each issue. You should be able to identify the key characteristics of each alternative — for example, how difficult or costly it would be to implement, how many of the issues in the case it would address, and what conflicts it might generate. Be sensitive to alternatives that are mutually exclusive or mutually supportive. Some steps would have to be taken at the same time in order for both to succeed; sometimes the opposite — taking two steps at the same time would negate both.

This is the part of case analysis where you can apply your creativity and knowledge. Your knowledge provides you with a set of possible responses; your creativity helps you recognize new applications for existing responses, potential variations on standard responses that would best fit the situation, and novel ways of addressing issues. One of the most serious blunders a case analyst can make is to jump immediately to a recommendation as "obvious" or "the only course of action possible" without exercising some creativity first. This is sometimes referred to as "ready, shoot, aim." You want to slow down before you pull the trigger, and make sure you have the correct target in your sights. Be careful, too, not to create "straw men" among your alternatives. Straw men in this context are alternatives developed for the sole purpose of rejecting them. A person reading your analysis should be able to see that the alternatives you have considered are reasonable and reasonably comprehensive. If your alternatives are not well thought out, why should we believe your recommendation is?

CONSEQUENCE EVALUATION

Once you have a list of alternatives, you must narrow the list down to one recommendation. To do this you must compare the consequences of each alternative and determine which one best meets the objectives of the decision maker. It is important at this point to consider both quantitative and qualitative outcomes. For example, strategic considerations sometimes require that the alternative with the best short-term financial outcome be rejected. It may be helpful at this stage to develop a set of criteria, based on the decision maker's objectives, to use in evaluating each alternative.

At this stage you may find there is no clear winner among your alternatives. Each of the alternatives may address a subset of the issues or have different cost/benefit tradeoffs. You may need to return to your earlier analysis and refine your identification of the objectives of your assignment or of the importance of various issues to ensure that you can identify the best alternative. You may also need to rethink your alternatives and ensure that you have been creative in considering what could be done. This is where "thinking outside the box" becomes valuable.

RECOMMENDATION

Once you have decided on the best alternative, you must present your recommendation to the decision maker. Your recommendation must be fully justified in terms of that person's objectives and capabilities. For example, if the company is a family business and the problem in the case is the incompetence of the controller (who is also the president's nephew), your recommendation must be sensitive to this detail. Your recommendation should make a convincing case for implementation based on the analysis you have performed. This is not the time to add additional reasons or details! The recommendation is a summary of your analysis, not another step in the analysis. If you find that you must introduce new material to justify your recommendation, you probably need to go back to your analysis and make sure you have done a thorough job.

IMPLEMENTATION ISSUES

Finally, you should consider how your recommendation will be implemented. In part you will have considered this issue in deciding which alternative to recommend, but depending on the case requirements, you may need to specify what will need to be done to implement your recommendation. This may involve, for example, indicating the order in which your recommendations should be implemented or what additional work — such as consultation with various parties or changes in operations — may be necessary to ensure success.

GROUP CASE ANALYSIS

It is very common to have students do case analyses in groups or teams. This approach to case analysis provides you with practice with the problem-solving approach that is typically used in business — cross-functional teams are brought together to deal with key problems. When a team functions effectively, it generates better alternatives and makes better recommendations than an individual. When a team does not function effectively, it can be a frustrating and emotionally draining experience. Here are some guidelines for helping your team produce an excellent case report:

1. *Be prepared.* Every member of the group must have done his/her reading and come to the group meeting prepared to participate.
2. *Take responsibility.* To use legal language, every member of the group is "joint and severally liable" for the outcome. In other words, every individual is responsible for the entire project. This has implications that are spelled out below. The group must establish very early what it expects of its members. If problems arise, they should be discussed and resolved within the group (this means moving the group to a higher level of functioning, not sweeping problems under the rug or reducing the team to a series of individual tasks).
3. *Challenge one another.* Although it may be convenient to assign tasks to different members of the group, *you* are responsible for the quality of the work done. All members must be willing to challenge one another (a) to ensure that each understands all the work that was done by the others, and (b) to be satisfied that the work meets everyone's standards of excellence. The final product must be a seamless report, not simply a merged set of individual documents. As a member of the team, you should be prepared to answer questions about any aspect of the final report, regardless of your specific contributions.
4. *Practise active listening.* To work effectively together, the team members must practise active listening skills. This means being open to others' opinions and respectful of differences; it also involves all the individual members providing feedback to demonstrate that they understand other members' positions and that everyone has been heard. When giving feedback, be specific and provide examples, and do so in a mutually supportive way, without being competitive or aggressive.

Group work is intended to improve the quality of case reports and the quality of the learning experience. It does so by exposing students to other perspectives and by encouraging them to develop key skills (such as leadership and follower skills, communication and negotiation skills, and organizational skills). Group work may not be the most efficient way to complete a task. It is used when the objective is to improve the quality of the work, not to get it done in the least amount of time. If your instructor has assigned a group case analysis, his/her expectations for the quality of the work will be higher than had the analysis been done by individuals. Keep this in mind!

WRITING A CASE ANALYSIS

The format of your case analysis will be specified in the "required" section of the case assignment. It may be a short memo that highlights the essential aspects of your analysis, a letter to communicate your findings to clients, or a comprehensive report that will be used to brief others who are responsible for making a decision based on your recommendation. Regardless of the format, your case write-up should be concise, well organized, logical, and persuasive.[2]

MEMO

A memo, or memorandum, is used to communicate between people in the same organization. This form of communication is typically shorter and less formal than a letter or report. A memo is concise, coherent, and sharply focused. It should include a brief introduction to frame the subject of the memo, a paragraph or paragraphs providing the body of the message, and, where appropriate, a brief conclusion. The conclusion may offer further help or contact information or simply be a courteous goodbye.

LETTER

A letter may contain the same information as a memo, but its tone tends to be more formal. It is often used to convey information outside the immediate work group, or where the information is being used by people outside the organization, such as customers or suppliers. Since it may be addressed to someone who does not have technical knowledge of the subject, great care must be taken to avoid jargon and to ensure that the meaning is unambiguous.

REPORT

Reports are used to communicate a comprehensive analysis of a case. Typically a report will include a letter (or memo) of transmittal that alerts the reader to the purpose of the report and its main conclusions or recommendations. A report's structure depends on its length and complexity, but a fairly long report typically contains a contents list, an executive summary, and an introduction, body, and conclusions. As appropriate, the report may include appendixes (typically for illustrative data or

---

[2] For a more comprehensive guide, see C. May and G.S. May, *Effective Writing: A Handbook for Accountants*, 4th ed. (Upper Saddle River, NJ: Prentice-Hall, 1996).

detailed calculations that would reduce the body text's readability if it were included there), a bibliography, and any figures or graphics to which the body text refers. The body of the report should provide enough detail that the reader can understand the logic and analysis that supports the development of alternatives and the recommendations or conclusions.

WHAT TO LOOK FOR IN A GOOD CASE ANALYSIS

Before leaving this chapter we want to stress once more that this guide to case analysis is not a checklist to be applied mechanically. Simply having headings that cover all the items discussed above and presenting your analysis in the format specified in the "required" section of the case will not make it a good case analysis. This guide reflects a set of principles about case analysis. A good case analysis is sensitive to the facts of the case; it interprets those facts using sound knowledge, identifies and prioritizes the issues facing the decision maker, creatively constructs and justifies alternatives, provides a recommendation based on a careful assessment of the costs and benefits of each alternative, and provides guidance for implementing the recommendation. A good case write-up provides evidence of the analysis process that you followed and is written clearly and persuasively.

Doing a good case analysis — in fact, doing a sound analysis of any business decision — is not easy! It requires a set of skills, which must be honed by practice and exercised with diligence and creativity. You will be able to develop these skills by using this book.

C H A P T E R 3

AN EXAMPLE CASE ANALYSIS

This chapter provides you with a sample case analysis. The case is presented in the same format as other cases in the book. It is followed by a response to the case written by the case author in the format a student would be expected to submit for an assignment or exam answer. This would be considered an "advanced case" similar to those in Chapter 5.

You may want to read the case and prepare your own response before reading the instructor's "solution." Remember that legitimate differences of opinion do arise in the analysis of cases and in the construction of alternatives and recommendations; the "solution" provided here is not the only correct answer to the case. Pay particular attention to how the case write-up identifies and discusses alternatives. This is a key aspect of the critical thinking skills you will develop while analyzing cases.

Again we emphasize that a case analysis must be tailored to fit its circumstances. In this chapter the assignment is to prepare a memo presenting a recommendation to your boss. As you read the response, focus on the process the author followed (identifying and prioritizing issues, generating alternatives, evaluating the consequences of the alternatives, making a recommendation, and where necessary pointing out implementation issues). Also, look for variations between the case solution and the generic model of case analysis presented in Chapter 2, and consider why the author modified the standard approach in this response.

If you treat the case solution in this chapter as a "case" to be analyzed, you will learn more about the process of case analysis than you would just from reading it as a "solution." In other words, study the solution to understand the process of case analysis; do not simply read it as a response to a particular case. To facilitate your understanding of the process of case analysis and write-up, we have annotated the solution with footnotes describing the essential aspects of the analysis and the key choices that were made. As you will see in these footnotes, the model of case analysis presented in Chapter 2 has been modified to fit the specifics of this case: some steps have been omitted or required very little work, and other steps are shown in detail. This reinforces the point made in Chapter 2: Do not apply the guide in a mechanical or checklist manner. Think about what each step is asking you to do and why. Each step contributes toward making a reasoned recommendation based on consideration of a range of alternatives. While the guidelines will help ensure that you have not missed anything in your case analysis, you must use them as principles to be modified to fit the nature of the case and the requirements of the analysis and write-up.

FAIRY FALLS: A TAXING QUESTION

Alan J. Richardson

Background

In Canada, the Constitution gives the federal and provincial governments the right to collect taxes to support their activities. The provinces, however, are restricted to "direct" taxes — that is, taxes that are paid by the person taxed and that cannot be passed on to others. This feature means that businesses cannot be taxed by the provinces in ways that are passed on to consumers. In several court cases,[1] businesses have successfully sued provincial and municipal governments (which are legal creations of the province and hence restricted to provincial powers) when permit and licensing fees have amounted to more than the costs associated with providing those services. Businesses have argued that the excess of a fee over the cost of providing services constitutes an indirect tax that will be passed on to consumers and thus is unconstitutional. Past court decisions suggest that the provinces (and municipalities) must ensure that all permit and licence fees reflect the actual cost of services.

Elizabeth Montgomery, the mayor of Fairy Falls,[2] a small community in Northern Ontario, has been reading summaries of these court cases. Although there is not yet a provincial requirement for municipalities to change the way they set fees, she is beginning to worry that the town may be in violation of the law. In addition, the Town Council has committed itself to sound financial management practices. As one way of meeting this commitment, it wants to make sure that it stays ahead of emerging issues. Since the town issues several thousand permits and licences each year, this could become a significant issue in the future. She has asked you, the Chief Administrative Officer (CAO), to provide an analysis and recommendation.

The Town of Fairy Falls

Fairy Falls is a small town in Muskoka, an area in Northern Ontario characterized by small lakes, a rugged, granite-strewn landscape, and tall pines. The population is widely dispersed and consists mainly of seasonal residents. The permanent population is about 5,000, but this increases to about 50,000 during the summer months as people move into vacation homes, trailer parks, and campgrounds. This means that the demand for municipal services, including permits and licences, varies dramatically during the year. A number of small businesses in the area (e.g., stores, motels, and fishing charters) cater to vacationers. There are also cranberry farms in the district, which are prospering. Fairy Falls is the administrative centre of this district.

---

[1] For example, *Ontario Home Builders' Association v. York Region Board of Education* [1996] 2 S.C.R. 929.

[2] This is a fictitious town and is not intended to represent real events or people. The costs shown in Table 3.1 are extracted from a real municipality for illustration purposes only.

The municipal office is located in a historic building in Fairy Falls that also houses a museum, as well as a visitors' centre operated by the Chamber of Commerce. The municipal operation is very lean, with the following full-time salaried personnel:

- The chief administrative officer, who also serves as economic development officer.
- The treasurer.
- The town clerk, who also serves as the municipal planner, and who issues licences for lotteries, temporary road closings, and pits and quarries.
- The bylaw enforcement officer, who monitors permits issued and who investigates reports of violations of municipal regulations.
- The development officer, who handles building permits, dock permits, septic permits, and so on. (Additional staff are brought in during the start of the construction season to ensure that buildings are not delayed by the approvals and inspections process.)

Fire services are provided by a volunteer fire department, which has a full-time fire chief, who provides training and who ensures that the equipment is maintained. The fire chief also issues burning permits during the fire season. Policing is handled by the Ontario Provincial Police under a long-term contract with the town.

The largest department, housed in a separate facility, is Public Works, which handles road repairs and maintenance, garbage and waste treatment, and the maintenance of parks and cemeteries. This department also maintains the town's water system and ensures that provincial regulations regarding water quality are met or exceeded at all times. This department works closely with the development officer to ensure that development permits are aligned with capital improvements to the town's infrastructure. The department has a Public Works Director and a permanent staff of five. Seasonal help is added during the summer to deal with road repairs and to provide services to seasonal residents, and during the winter to deal with snow removal. In spring and fall this department shrinks in size.

Permits and Licensing

The main permits/licences issued by the town on a routine basis are:

- building permits,
- dock permits,
- septic permits,
- burn permits,
- lottery and Bingo licences, *and*
- licences to operate pits and quarries.

The town has never had a formal policy regarding the amounts to be charged for permits and licences. Generally, the fees have been set by the Town Council on the recommendation of the CAO. The fees were originally set to be comparable to those of neighbouring municipalities; this was to ensure that the amounts did not impede business development. The fee increases that have been approved by the Town Council have tended to match increases in the town's overall expenditures and have averaged 3 percent per year over the past decade, although some fees, such as dog licences, have not changed for a decade. Some of the fees charged are listed in Table 1.

TABLE 1: Examples of Permit and Licence Fees

Purpose	Administered by	Fee charged	Comments
Bingo Licence	Town Clerk	3% of the total prizes awarded	
Road Closing Permit	Town Clerk	$500 per application	$250 refunded if the application fails
Transient Trader Licence	Town Clerk	$300 per vendor	
Dog Licence	Town Clerk	$10 per dog	
Trailer Camp Licence	Development Officer	$200 for initial application; $100 per year annual fee plus $10 per trailer site	
Taxi Cab Licence	Town Clerk	$50 for the first vehicle; $15 for each additional vehicle	
Building Permits	Development Officer	$7.00 per $1,000 of value	Minimum fee $100
Sewer System Permit	Development Officer	$300 for new systems; $150 for an existing system; $100 for reinspection after failure	
Development Charges	Development Officer	$2,013 flat fee for residential buildings; $0.57 per square foot for commercial buildings	
Burn Permit	Fire Department	$50 per year	

These examples are taken, for illustrative purposes only, from The Township of Muskoka Lakes http://www. township.muskokalakes.on.ca/Pdfs/Other%20Pdfs/List%20of%20Municipal%20Fees.2005.pdf.

Source: Reprinted with permission of the Corporation of the Township of Muskoka Lakes, www.township.muskokalakes.on.ca.

Required

Prepare a memo to the mayor that analyzes the following:

- The town's current compliance with the court's view of appropriate permit and licence fees.
- If you believe the town is not in compliance, where you believe changes should be made, and how these changes should be made.
- Any additional issues that would arise if fees were changed.

CASE ANALYSIS AND RECOMMENDATION[3]

To: Mayor, Fairy Falls[4]

From: Chief Administrative Officer, Fairy Falls

Re: Review of Permit and Licence Fees

I have reviewed the current structure of our licence and permit fees in light of your concerns about recent court decisions. I believe that we are not in compliance with the court's directive that these fees must reflect the actual cost of providing the services. In the memo below I will identify some potential problem areas, prioritize where we should make changes, and recommend a plan for undertaking these changes. I recommend that we undertake an activity-based costing study of the cost of providing permits and licences, beginning with those affecting businesses.

A Review of Current Fee Structures

It is unlikely that our present system of permit and licensing fees reflects the costs of these services.[5] First, we know that these fees were originally set based on the fees used by neighbouring municipalities. We did not use our costs at that time as a basis for setting fees. Second, the fees have been adjusted periodically with across-the-board percentage increases. Unless each permit and licensing process uses exactly the same resources, it is unlikely that the costs associated with different products would increase at the same rate. Finally, a quick review of our permit and licence fees shows a variety of pricing models:

- variable fees (e.g., Bingo licences, building permits)

- fixed fees (e.g., dog licences, transient trader licences, road closing permits)

- combination fixed and variable fees (e.g., trailer camp licences, taxi cab licences)

---

[3] This is an example response to the case; other approaches may be possible.

[4] The response format chosen is a memo as this is a communication within the organization. The addressee is the mayor, but it is likely that the document will be shared with other members of council and possibly a wider public. This context means that the discussion must be presented in lay terms (i.e., no jargon should be used, and technical terms must be explained) and that care must be taken to set out options for the mayor and council to discuss and decide upon.

[5] In this case the issue has been identified by the mayor but the analysis first tries to judge whether or not this issue is actually present. If, for example, the CAO historically based recommendations for fees on costs, then the mayor's issue would disappear. This discussion provides three case facts that indicate the likelihood that a problem exists.

It seems unlikely, on the face of it, that these patterns of fees reflect the underlying pattern of costs. For example, our Bingo licence fee varies with the value of the prize, but it seems likely that the cost of issuing and policing the licence is virtually the same for each Bingo. In addition, some of our fees recur annually (e.g., trailer camp licences) and we may not be providing an annual service that justifies these fees.

Overall, I believe that the relationship between our costs and our fees is subject to challenge. Furthermore, at present we would not be able to provide a cost-based justification for these fees.

Issues in Identifying Costs

Any attempt to link costs and fees will have to recognize some technical issues owing to the size of the municipality and the nature of the services we provide:[6]

- First, because of the seasonality of municipal operations, actual costs may vary depending on the time of year a service is provided. For example, in winter we may approve only one or two building permits per month, whereas in spring we receive hundreds of applications per month.[7] We need to decide whether we want to charge the actual cost of providing a service or the average cost over the year, as these costs will vary with the volume of work done.

- Second, we are a small municipality but we are required by law to provide basic services to our residents. This means that there are fixed costs associated with our activities (e.g., we have a full-time Town Clerk whose salary does not vary depending on the number of permits issued), so the extra cost of processing a licensing application in this situation is zero (since we would have to pay the clerk's salary regardless of whether the application was made). This means that the marginal cost of providing services will differ dramatically from the full or average cost. We need to decide whether we want to charge the full cost of providing permits and licences or the marginal cost.

---

[6] These are situational constraints that will affect how costs can be estimated and that will establish a second issue — that "cost" does not refer to a single number so that linking fees to "cost" also means choosing which cost to use for this purpose.

[7] This is not a fact in the case, but rather a reasonable assumption given the seasonality of construction in Canada.

Alternatives

A number of alternatives are available to Council that would address the problems raised by the court cases. These alternatives are discussed below in more detail.[8] The alternatives follow:

- Do nothing.

- Rearrange operations to make the costs of permits and licences visible.

- Undertake a costing study to identify the costs of permits and licences under current operations. This option allows for two main variations regarding how the costs are to be calculated:

  - Calculate full versus marginal costs.

  - Calculate actual versus average (normal) costs.

One alternative is to do nothing. At the moment, while there are court rulings on the relationship between costs and fees, these are specific to particular instances and there is no requirement for us to act at this time. However, I appreciate that you, as Mayor, want to keep the Town at the forefront of municipal financial management, and it makes sense to anticipate the risk of court challenges to our fees.[9] I believe that we should be proactive in addressing this issue.

If we decide to act to align our costs with our fees, then we have two alternatives. First, we can arrange our activities so that the costs of providing permits and licences are directly attributable to those processes.[10] This will make the costs visible and will meet the concerns regarding the relationship between costs and fees. Second, we can do cost studies to identify the costs of these activities as we are presently organized.

---

[8] The memo is designed as a decision tree to show the mayor what alternatives are available. The choices at the higher levels of the tree are policy decisions that should be taken by political representatives. The choices at lower levels of the tree are more technical decisions that the council would be happy to delegate to the staff.

[9] This sentence recognizes the mayor's objectives in undertaking the review and uses this to reject the alternative of doing nothing until challenged in the courts. This brief paragraph combines alternative generation, consequence evaluation, and a decision with regard to further consideration of the alternative.

[10] Many costing problems arise because the way a business is structured disguises the costs incurred. It is not unusual for a business to reorganize so that costs can be more easily recognized and managed. For example, firms may outsource services because of the lack of good internal information to judge their efficiency and effectiveness.

I do not believe that we can or should establish separate units for permits and licences. Since we are a small municipality, many of our resources are shared among different functions. In addition, our permitting and licencing functions are spread among (at least) three different departments to take advantage of the specialized expertise associated with each department. We would not have the scale of operations to create separate units in each department to handle permits and licences, and we do not have people with the range of skills and knowledge needed to bring all of these functions together in one unit. These constraints make the creation of a separate unit, or units, to deal with permits and licences an inefficient way of handling the issue.

This discussion supports the alternative of developing a costing system to capture the costs of permits and licences. There are many choices that can be made in designing a costing system, most of which are technical details that our staff will handle. There are two main choices, however, that you as Mayor and the Council may wish to consider.[11] First, we must decide whether we will charge the actual costs of each permit, or an average cost that ignores variations in cost over the year and that also ignores *minor* (the meaning of "minor" will be discussed below) variations in the specifics of a permit or licence application. Second, we need to decide whether we will calculate the full cost or the marginal cost of our services. I believe that we should be calculating the average (normal), full costs of permits and licences.

It would be expensive to calculate the actual costs of providing services (i.e., each permit or licence application would be billed according to the resources used), and these costs would vary widely over the year, resulting in incentives for people to delay their applications for permits and licences until the busiest times of year, since the higher volume of activity would result in lower costs during those periods based on economies of scale. Also, our citizens expect to be treated equally by their municipality, and the cost of a permit should not vary depending on factors beyond their control.[12] This suggests that we should find the average cost of permits and licences and set fees according to this cost. The only variation in these costs should relate to

---

[11] The way the memo is formatted depends heavily on the role being taken. In this case the response from the CAO to the mayor crosses a line between operational and strategic issues. The response must identify the issues that have political consequences and leave those to the council, while identifying minor issues that will be handled internally.

[12] These two criteria are being introduced to help narrow the alternatives. The criteria are not explicit in the case but are reasonable given the context (i.e., a municipal government in which the usual rules regarding equal treatment of all citizens would apply).

factors that the applicant can control. For example, a permit for a complex activity that requires hours of work by staff to review should be charged more than a simple permit, but the same permit submitted at different times of the year should not be charged differently. The costing study should help us identify which characteristics of permit and licence applications cause us to incur more costs, and which variations can be considered minor and thus can be ignored in establishing our fee schedule.

Since in total our revenues must cover the expenses of the municipality, and the marginal cost of some resources involved in providing any single licence or permit may be zero, the use of marginal costing would not allow us to fund the capacity needed to provide our services.[13] Full costing would ensure that we *can* cover these costs. This requires that we allocate a portion of our fixed costs (e.g., staff time) to permits and licences. There are many cost allocation procedures that could be used for this purpose. Once you and the Council have agreed on the basis on which our costs should be calculated, the staff and I will design an appropriate system. Given the discussion above, however, it would be useful to follow allocation procedures that are based on the attributes of applications that cause variations in our cost of providing the service. Activity-based costing is one approach that focuses on the processes that generate costs, and it would fit well with this situation.[14] This is probably the approach that we would use if the recommendation below is accepted.

Recommendation

I recommend that we conduct an activity-based costing (ABC) analysis to determine the average full costs of our services. An ABC analysis will identify the time spent by staff and the resources consumed to complete the processing of permits and licensing applications. The ABC analysis will begin by identifying the processes that are undertaken (e.g., hours of development officer time spent on a building permit review), and

---

[13] This point could be expanded to ensure that the distinction is clear. At the margin, each additional application requires no new resources, so in essence the cost of providing the service (the opportunity cost) is zero. But if we don't charge for any application, then we would have no funds to hire the people who provide those services (this is the classic public good problem in economics). The solution suggested here is to charge people in order to have the capacity available to process the application. This requires us to know the expected or average number of applications during the year and calculate the average cost accordingly.

[14] A judgment is required regarding how much detail about alternatives to present. In this response, the alternatives shown are those which will dramatically affect the fees charged and the likelihood that the fees will support the long-run cost of the services and be acceptable to the citizens (i.e., full versus marginal costs, actual versus normal costs). These alternatives are important to the mayor and council. The details of ABC are not important, but presenting this alternative in brief demonstrates how the costing will be implemented.

identify the costs of those processes (e.g., the portion of the salary of the development officer for the time spent), and then accumulate the costs to show the average full cost of our services. The process analysis will also show whether there are variations in the nature of permits and licence applications that affect our costs and that should be reflected in our fee schedules. Although this approach requires judgment and represents an approximation of how resources will be consumed in the long run, assuming no changes in the underlying processes, it is systematic and well documented and thus will support any legal defence of our fees should this be necessary.[15]

Implementation Issues

Prior to undertaking the costing studies, I cannot say whether the costs of permits and licences will increase or decrease. This has two consequences that the Council should recognize.[16] First, since permit and licence fees are part of the municipality's revenues, a change in the fees charged may result in either a reduction or an increase in the other taxes we charge in order to make the changes revenue neutral overall (i.e., any increase or decrease in permit fees must be offset by a change in other taxes or by a change in expenses). Council should be aware of the political implications of this change.

Second, the changes in fees charged may affect the competitiveness of our permits relative to those of neighbouring municipalities. If these changes are material, it may have positive or negative impacts on business decisions (e.g., builders may find it more or less expensive to build speculative homes in Fairy Falls if the cost of building permits, septic permits, and the like changes materially).

Since the possibility of court challenges to our fees by business was the initial motivation for your request, I also recommend that we begin this process with a study of those permits which are of largest absolute value and which have the most impact on

---

[15] This last sentence brings the recommendation back to the mayor's concern about the legal risk to which the town may be exposed by using fees that cannot be justified based on cost.

[16] The context of this case is important. The role of the CAO is to implement the policies of the Council, but the CAO needs also to apprise Council of any actions that may result in concerns by taxpayers. The Council represents taxpayers and needs to make decisions with their interests in mind, but in some cases decisions need to be taken that will have unavoidable impacts on taxpayers. In these cases the Council's role is to ensure that the need for the action is understood and that potential opposition to the plan is managed to allow the staff to function effectively.

businesses. I would prioritize building (and related) permits and business operating licences. Minor permits such as burn permits and dog licences can be left until more staff time is available for analysis.

One side effect of generating better information about the costs of our permits and licences is that we will be able to manage those costs. I recommend that we put in place an activity-based management system to help ensure that we are providing these services as efficiently as possible, and that we benchmark our fees against those of other municipalities that have made the change to cost-based fee schedules.

CHAPTER 4

INTRODUCTORY CASES

The cases in this book have been divided into two chapters and labelled as introductory and advanced. Cases from either chapter could be used in an introductory management accounting course. The differences between the two sets of cases relate to the degree of emphasis on calculations and the range of issues addressed in each case.

The following introductory cases are more focused and rely more on quantitative analysis for making recommendations. It is important to recognize, however, that even when quantitative analysis is used, choices must still be made. Quantitative analysis is used to answer questions and evaluate alternatives. Before undertaking the analysis, make sure that you have thought carefully about the issues in the case, identified the alternatives that should be considered, and used the quantitative analysis to help understand the consequences of those alternatives and to justify your recommendations. Also, you should recognize that there may be alternative tools that could be used in your analysis as well as alternative ways of specifying the problem to be analyzed with a given tool. Be sure that you have considered these issues and can explain why you have chosen a particular analytic tool.

BEDFORD PROPERTY MANAGEMENT: VARIANCE ANALYSIS

Prem Lobo

Bedford Property Management ("Bedford") is a facilities management company with operations across the country. The owners of office buildings contract Bedford to perform all maintenance functions for their buildings. Tenants in office buildings phone Bedford when a service problem arises such as a malfunctioning elevator, a burned-out light, or a broken furnace. Bedford dispatches a service team to address the problem and charges the property owner for the service call. The number of service calls received by Bedford fluctuates over the year: calls peak during the summer months and decline toward the Christmas holidays. Bedford guarantees that service issues will be addressed within 3 hours of a tenant phoning in about a problem. This policy has given Bedford an edge over its competition.

Some service jobs take more time than others. At the start of each year, Bedford creates an annual budget for revenues, direct expenses, and fixed costs. Variances are calculated between actual results and budget on a monthly basis.

In December, Bedford received and responded to 10,000 service requests. It billed clients at an average rate of $100 per service call. December's budget called for 15,000 service requests to be processed at an average rate of $110 per job. The monthly budget figures reflect annual figures divided by 12.

For each service job, Bedford budgets 2 hours of direct labour at $25 per hour. In December, Bedford actually incurred 25,000 hours of labour at $30 per hour.

For December, Bedford budgeted for fixed overhead of $100,000. Monthly budget figures for fixed overhead reflect annual figures divided by 12. Fixed overhead includes such expenses as heating and electricity at Bedford's head office, and maintenance on Bedford's service equipment (which is usually carried out in December). Actual overhead expenses incurred for December were $125,000.

Ms. Kim is the general manager of Bedford's operations. When she was hired in November, the president instructed her to "run a tight ship . . . cost overruns from budget must be eliminated in any way possible, including by downsizing our service staff." Ms. Kim is a little apprehensive because early indications are that December was not a great month for Bedford. However, she is not quite sure whether Bedford's results actually reflect reality. She is also uncertain about which performance variances she ought to be held accountable for. She has hired you to calculate variances from budget and help her analyze them.

Required

1. Calculate appropriate variances to understand Bedford's performance. Then suggest potential causes for these variances, and identify which variances Ms. Kim should be accountable for.
2. Do the calculated variances adequately capture Bedford's performance? Explain. Specifically identify any concerns you have with respect to the calculated variance figures and what they imply. What steps should Ms. Kim take in responding to these variances?

TECHNICAL SUPPORT DIVISION

Tony Dimnik

Zorka Dubay is the manager of the Technical Support Division of Information Technology International (ITI). ITI contracts with various organizations to provide technical support for their computer and information systems. Technicians are assigned to work with each organization and are often located in rented facilities near the client. Technicians are essentially independent contractors and are paid only for the work they do. Each team of assigned technicians is called a "group," and results are evaluated on the basis of "cost per hour of billed service" for the group.

Zorka looks over the July results and notices that the four-technician group assigned to Industry Canada in Ottawa significantly exceeded its budgeted cost per hour that month. As Table 1 shows, the actual cost per hour of $73.30 was $8.37 more than the budgeted $64.93.

Zorka wonders why the cost per hour was so high.

TABLE 1: Industry Canada Group Results for July 2005

	Original budget	Actual results	Variances (actual–original)
Hours billed by technicians	552	460	−92
Average hourly rate for technicians	45	47	2
Technical services salaries	24,840	21,620	−3,220
Telecommunications	3,000	2,900	−100
Rent and utilities	8,000	9,200	1,200
Total	**$35,840**	**$33,720**	**−2,120**
Cost per hour of billed service	**$64.93**	**$73.30**	**8.37**

Required

Prepare a memo explaining why the cost per hour exceeded expectations.

TRYBEE INC.

Tony Dimnik

Trybee Inc. manufactures and sells bicycles and tricycles. This small company is organized into five departments. Following is a brief description of each of the departments:

- *Administration* — The president of Trybee and her staff are responsible for finance, planning, marketing, and sales.
- *Human Resources* — The HR Department does the hiring and payroll for the other four departments. The direct costs of HR include departmental salaries, office supplies, telephones, and computers.
- *Janitorial* — The janitorial staff service the other four departments but spend most of their time cleaning and maintaining the areas occupied by the two manufacturing departments: Assembly and Painting. The direct costs of this department include departmental salaries, supplies, and equipment.
- *Assembly* — This department assembles bikes and trikes from parts purchased from outside suppliers. Assembly workers record their hours for payroll purposes and also indicate whether their time was spent working on bikes or on trikes. Although this department occupies twice the space of the Painting Department, the janitorial staff spend little time here because everything is kept well ordered and clean.
- *Painting* — This department spray-paints the assembled bikes and trikes. Just as in the Assembly Department, the workers here record the hours they spend on bikes and trikes. The space occupied by this department is messy and dirty and requires a lot of attention from the janitorial staff.

Product Costing

Table 1 summarizes the direct costs, occupied space, and head count for each of the departments as well as the direct costs, revenues, and number of units of bikes and trikes. Figure 1 shows how costs are assumed to flow from department to department and ultimately to the two products: bikes and trikes.

Trybee's management has been considering two alternative approaches to costing products. Under alternative 1, administration costs would be allocated to HR and Janitorial based on floor area, and the costs of HR and Janitorial would be allocated to Assembly and Painting based on floor area. The costs of Assembly and Painting would be allocated to bikes and trikes based on revenue.

Under alternative 2, Administration costs would be allocated to HR and Janitorial based on head count, and the costs of HR and Janitorial would be allocated to Assembly and Painting based on head count. The costs of Assembly and Painting would be allocated to bikes and trikes based on the number of units produced.

TABLE 1: Annual Costs and Revenues for Trybee

	Direct costs	Floor space (m²)	Head count	Revenue	Units
Administration	$100	50	5	—	—
HR	200	30	4	—	—
Janitorial	150	20	6	—	—
Assembly	300	200	8	—	—
Painting	250	100	12	—	—
Bikes	500	—	—	$1,500	50
Trikes	400	—	—	1,000	200
Totals	**1,900**	—	—	**2,500**	**250**

FIGURE 1: Cost Allocations for Trybee

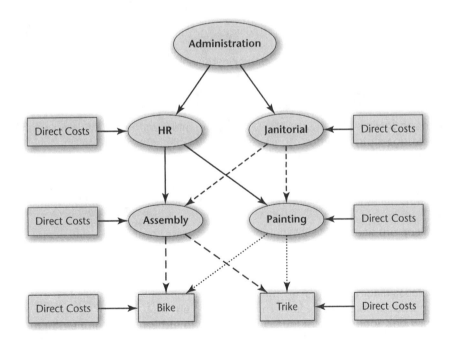

Required

1. Calculate the cost of one bike and one trike under alternative 1 and under alternative 2.
2. Calculate the per unit and total profitability of each product under alternative 1 and alternative 2.

3. If at the end of the year, after all the bikes and trikes have been sold, a customer were to ask Trybee to manufacture one more bike and one more trike, what would be the cost of each of these units?

4. The president is considering contracting out janitorial services. What is the annual cost of the Janitorial Department?

ENTERON CORPORATION: PERFORMANCE EVALUATION

Prem Lobo

Jeff Gillick, the CEO of Enteron Inc., sighs as he examines the performance of three of Enteron's divisions. In 2006 the Development Division recorded another good year, with actual profits exceeding budget by 25 percent. Meanwhile, the Operations Division recorded a loss for the year, a shortfall of 30 percent from budgeted profits. The Gas Division recorded the best performance of all three, with profits 75 percent in excess of budget.

Jeff is puzzled by the wide profit variances among his divisions. Each division is a profit centre, with the respective divisional manager receiving a bonus based on profitability. At present the Gas Division will receive the biggest bonus. However, before finalizing bonuses, Jeff wants you, as a consultant, to review the variances and identify potential issues. In particular, he notes: "I want to be sure that our division managers receive bonuses for the right reasons. I don't want my managers to be punished — or rewarded — unfairly."

You learn the following:

Development Division

- This division constructs power stations in Asia, South America, and Eastern Europe.
- A typical power station takes two years to build. Once constructed, the power stations are "sold" internally to the Operations Division, with the difference between the sale price and the construction cost being reported as profit by the Development Division.
- Enteron's corporate management has set a predetermined price for the sale of power stations from the Development Division to the Operations Division. The larger the power station, the higher the predetermined price.
- The Development Division has been developing mostly large-scale power stations. This division has been in the news lately owing to an extremely large power station in Asia that has resulted in environmental concerns.

Operations Division

- This division buys power stations constructed by Enteron's Development Division and operates them. It generates revenue by selling electricity produced to customers, and it incurs operating costs.
- The Operations Division is required by corporate rules to purchase all power stations constructed by the Development Division.
- New power stations typically take four years to reach profitability. Larger power stations take much longer.
- The division's largest power station was shut down for a number of months in 2006 because of damage caused by an employee error. The employee had not received sufficient training.

Gas Division

- The Gas Division supplies natural gas to factories in Europe and North America.
- During 2006 this division entered into a complex sales agreement with a large commercial customer. The agreement guaranteed the customer a supply of gas at a substantially discounted price over a 20-year period. As per GAAP financial accounting rules, the division recorded the discounted present value of the all future revenues during 2006.
- The price of gas tends to be volatile.
- Gas prices have increased 50 percent over the past 10 years.

Required

Prepare a report to the CEO, discussing the profit variances of the divisions in relation to the information provided. Identify any issues he should be concerned about before he assesses the performance of each division's managers.

POTTER INC.: COST ALLOCATION

Prem Lobo

Potter Inc. is a manufacturer of broomsticks. It manufactures two models — the Nimblus and the Fireboldt. The Nimblus model is made by the Nimblus Division and the Fireboldt by the Fireboldt Division. Each division has a vice president who oversees sales generation and manufacturing operations.

A recent recession has led to a decline in broomstick sales, and Potter has had difficulty staying profitable. Potter has begun examining its cost allocation policies in the hope of improving decision making at the company. The company has hired you, a consultant, to assist senior management in this regard.

In discussions with Potter's controller, you learn the following with respect to the company's cost allocation practices:

- Direct materials, direct labour, and variable overhead costs are currently allocated[1] to the two divisions based on the number of manufacturing labour hours incurred. Each model of broomstick uses relatively the same number of labour hours. The Fireboldt uses more expensive materials and requires more supervisor time than the Nimblus model.

- Fixed overhead includes rent, utilities, and taxes. It also includes the costs of manufacturing support departments, which provide services to both divisions. These departments include quality control, repairs and maintenance, and materials purchasing. At present, fixed overhead costs are not allocated to each division; rather, they appear as period expenses on Potter's financial statements.

- Product support costs include advertising, research and development, and legal and professional services. These costs are currently not allocated to each division; instead, like fixed overhead, they appear as period expenses on Potter's income statements.

The controller tells you: "We allocate variable production costs to our products because that's the way we do things for financial accounting purposes. Our financial accounting income statements are prepared on a direct costing basis, with only variable costs allocated to inventory. We find it convenient to use financial accounting information for management decision making."

You also learn the following:

- *Performance evaluation* — The Nimblus and Fireboldt Divisions are evaluated as profit centres, with their respective vice presidents receiving a bonus based on meeting or exceeding budgeted profit levels.

- *Product pricing* — Potter sets selling prices for the Nimbus and the Fireboldt using a cost-plus pricing policy. The policy's aim is to charge a high enough price to cover total product costs and also generate a profit.

---

[1] In this case materials and labour are being treated as indirect costs and allocated to products. This is an unusual situation but sometimes used when these costs are a small portion of total costs and do not vary materially across products.

- *Support services* — To help each division attain its sales and profit goals, Potter maintains a common quality-control, repairs and maintenance, and materials purchasing department. Last year, support costs experienced a significant increase; as a result, some employees had to be laid off to reduce costs.
- *Special orders* — Customers sometimes contact each division with requests for small quantities of broomsticks for one-time discounted prices. In the past, the divisions have agreed to such special orders as long as the selling price charged is enough to cover the allocated production costs.

Required

Prepare a memo to Potter's controller that critiques Potter's cost allocation practices. Be sure to discuss the impact of the existing cost allocation system on management decision making by using specific examples. If applicable, suggest ways that Potter could change or improve the way it allocates costs.

SPARKY INC.: COST ALLOCATION

Prem Lobo

Sparky Inc. manufactures and sells gizmos. Sparky's manufacturing operations are organized into one quality control department and three production departments — A, B, and C, respectively. Each production department manufactures a different brand of gizmos. The quality control department provides checks for each of the three production departments.

Each production department is treated as a cost centre. The respective managers are awarded year-end performance bonuses on the basis of meeting budgeted costs or achieving cost savings. All costs incurred by the quality control department are allocated to production departments using the number of quality control ("QC") checks as an allocation base.

When planning for the 2006 fiscal year, Sparky's senior management budgeted for total QC department costs of $1,000 and total QC checks of 100 for a budgeted cost allocation rate of $10 per QC check. A, B, and C were expected to demand 50, 30, and 20 QC checks respectively.

Actual costs incurred by the QC department during 2006 were $1,265, and actual QC jobs demanded by A, B, and C were 50, 50, and 15, respectively, resulting in total costs allocated to A, B, and C of $550, $550, and $165, respectively. Because of increased demand for QC services, the QC department incurred overtime expenses.

During performance evaluations at year end, the manager of A expressed serious misgivings about the costs allocated to her division: "I don't think our cost allocation system is fair. Why should I be held accountable for someone else's efficiency or someone else's level of consumption?"

Required

Address the concerns of A's manager — specifically, consider whether Sparky's cost allocation system is fair. What alternatives could you suggest to improve the way costs are allocated and performances evaluated at Sparky?

SPECIFIC ELECTRIC INC.: TRANSFER PRICING

Prem Lobo

Specific Electric Inc. (SEI) has two divisions: Division A and Division B. Each division is treated as a profit centre and is evaluated based on whether it meets or exceeds budgeted profits for the year. The managers of each division have considerable freedom to make business decisions that affect the revenues and expenses of their divisions.

Division A manufactures generators, all of which are sold for industrial use. Division B manufactures dynamos, which are usually sold to external customers as components for electrical machinery. Although dynamos are used in manufacturing generators, Division A normally purchases dynamos from a competitor of Division B.

At present, SEI does not require internal transfers between divisions. However, SEI policies decree that when internal transfers do occur, they should occur at "market," with market defined as the selling division's external sale price.

The following information pertains to SEI's two divisions:

Division A

Per unit selling price to external third-party customers	$ 100
Cost of dynamos purchased from external sources	60
Other production costs	20
Profit margin per generator	$ 20

Division B

Per unit selling price to external third-party customers	$ 80
Per unit production costs	35
Other variable costs per unit	15
Profit margin per dynamo	$ 30

In addition:

- Other variable costs per unit incurred by Division B include $5 per unit for shipping and $5 per unit for sales commissions. If product were to be sold internally, these costs would be saved.
- Division B has a production capacity of 100,000 units per year. Some years, production runs at full capacity, other years, at less than full capacity.

SEI's vice president of operations is proposing a review of the company's transfer pricing policy in order to enhance goal-congruent decision making by its divisions. The vice president has hired you, a consultant, to perform this review. Specifically, she would like your review to focus on the following:

- Whether Division A and Division B should engage in internal transfers, and in what situations.
- What range of transfer prices the two divisions could transact.

- Whether the two divisions would want to engage in internal transfers, given the existing market-based transfer pricing policy.
- Whether the existing market-based transfer pricing policy will result in goal-congruent decisions on the part of Divisions A and B.
- What alternative transfer-pricing policies might enhance goal-congruent decision making by divisions.

Required

Perform the review for the vice president of operations, explaining your logic fully and supporting your analysis with any assumptions and/or calculations you consider necessary.

TANYA LAWN EQUIPMENT INC.: TRANSFER PRICING

Prem Lobo

Tanya Lawn Equipment Inc. manufactures gasoline-powered lawn equipment such as lawn mowers and trimmers, as well as motors for use in appliances such as lawn mowers and chain saws, among other products.

Division A is part of Tanya and manufactures various models of lawn mowers and trimmers. This division is evaluated as a profit centre. It has identified a new opportunity to manufacture and sell leaf blowers in addition to its existing products.

Division A's management has determined that the new leaf blowers will be priced at $150 per unit, will require $20 per unit of variable costs, and will be allocated $30 per unit of fixed overhead. The leaf blower will also require a motor, which will have to be purchased by Division A. The division's management would like to find a reliable supplier for the motors. Once such a supplier has been identified, the division plans to sign it to a 3-year supply contract.

Division A has received price quotations from three external suppliers for the required motor: $50, $55, and $60 per unit. All three potential suppliers have been eager to offer attractive prices in order to land Division A's business.

However, Division A's management is somewhat surprised to learn that another division of Tanya — Division B — specializes in manufacturing the same kind of motor that the new leaf blower will require. Division B usually sells its motors for $65 per unit. Variable costs are $45 per unit, and allocated fixed overhead is $10 per unit.

Division B has a good reputation among its customers and usually operates at full capacity. However, as it turns out, Division B has enough excess capacity during this current year to supply Division A's requirement for motors. This is because one of Division B's largest customers experienced a strike during the year and thus did not purchase as many motors as it usually does. This strike has since been resolved, and normal purchase levels will resume next year. Division B is a profit centre.

Required

1. From the perspective of Tanya as a whole, should Division A purchase the motors from Division B or from one of the three external suppliers? Discuss, with full reasoning, the various issues that would have to be considered.

2. Tanya's policy states that any internal transfers between divisions should be made at the midpoint between the selling division's cost and the buying division's external purchase price (i.e., the price an external buyer can purchase for). Under this policy, will Division A and B transact? Is this a goal-congruent solution for Tanya?

UNIONVILLE HEART CENTRE

Prem Lobo

The Unionville Heart Centre (the "Heart Centre") is a small, government-funded hospital operating in Ontario that specializes in heart surgery.

Surgeries performed by the hospital are billed to the government at a predetermined rate pursuant to the Ontario Health Insurance Plan (OHIP). However, the recently elected provincial government has announced that it may "privatize" health care in the near future so that hospitals will be free to charge patients directly for services performed. The issue of privatization has been debated quite a bit in the media recently and would constitute a significant change in the health care industry.

The Heart Centre performs three types of heart surgery: heart transplants, valve replacements, and bypass surgery. The Heart Centre is the only hospital in the province and one of the few in the country offering heart transplants and valve replacement procedures. In 2004 it performed 50 transplants, 100 valve replacements, and 250 bypass procedures at a total cost of $10,000,000, or $25,000 per procedure. These costs are broken down as follows:

Direct costs of surgery (medication, bandages, materials, etc.)	$1,000,000
Indirect costs of surgery	
Salaries of medical professionals	$5,000,000
Building maintenance costs	1,000,000
Laboratory costs	2,000,000
Administration	1,000,000
	$9,000,000

The government has criticized the Heart Centre for having what it calls an "excessive" cost per procedure of $25,000 and has threatened to reduce its funding unless this is "rectified." The government has compared the Heart Centre to three other hospitals in the province that perform heart procedures and that, on average, reported a total cost per procedure of $15,000.

During a recent staff meeting, the hospital's management expressed its concern about budget cutbacks and asked staff to identify ways to reduce expenditures. Doug Howser, a recently hired management accountant, surprised everyone by speaking up and saying: "I don't believe that our costs are excessive at all. I think the problem lies in how costs per procedure are being calculated. I think we should use an ABC analysis to calculate the costs for each type of surgery. When we do so, I'm sure this will reveal a completely different picture."

To support his case, Doug presented some preliminary information (see Exhibit 1).

Hospital management did not place much credence in what Doug had to say and was not inclined to take his suggestions into account. The CEO stated: "A full ABC cost system is too expensive. At present, our goal is to try and save on costs. In addition, ABC is really used for product pricing and not much else, so we would be wasting our time and money implementing ABC here."

EXHIBIT 1: Information to Perform an ABC Analysis

Cost item	Total cost	Cost driver
Direct costs	$1,000,000	Number of surgeries performed
Indirect costs		
Medical salaries	$5,000,000	Number of professional hours worked
Building maintenance	1,000,000	Square footage utilized (Note <1>)
Laboratory costs	2,000,000	Number of laboratory reports requested (Note <2>)
Administration	1,000,000	1/3 allocated equally to each of transplants, valve replacements, and bypass

Note <1> Alternate cost driver: number of maintenance jobs carried out
Note <2> Alternate cost driver: Hours of laboratory time taken

Cost Driver Information for the year 2004

	Transplants	Valve replacements	Bypass	Total
Total number of surgeries	50	100	250	400
Professional hours worked	2,000	3,000	5,000	10,000
Square footage utilized	30,000	10,000	10,000	50,000
Number of maintenance jobs	600	210	190	1,000
Laboratory reports requested	200	200	250	650
Total laboratory hours	1,000	300	700	2,000

Required

Perform a preliminary ABC analysis, using the information presented in Exhibit 1 to determine the cost to perform each surgical procedure. Explain clearly your assumptions as well as any issues you may have with the information compiled in Exhibit 1. What does the ABC analysis reveal about the cost per procedure? How does this compare with the previously determined cost per procedure? What insights, if any, does this analysis reveal with respect to the Heart Centre's activities?

Is hospital management correct to state that a full ABC system would not be worthwhile? Discuss, with reference to various contexts, and stating any assumptions you consider necessary.

WRIGHT INDUSTRIES

Prem Lobo

Wright Industries operates across Canada. Wright is a mature company and has two divisions: Widget and Gizmo. The Widget Division has been granted a monopoly to manufacture and sell widgets in Canada. The Gizmo Division is a retailer of gizmos and operates in a highly competitive market.

The summarized financial statements for the Widget and Gizmo divisions for 2007 are presented below (in $000s):

	Widget division (monopoly)	Gizmo division (competitive)
Revenues	$1,000,000	$500,000
Variable costs	500,000	400,000
Gross margin	500,000	100,000
Fixed costs	100,000	50,000
Profit	**$400,000**	**$50,000**
Profit margin	40%	10%

Recently, Canada experienced a recession. Alpha Corporation, a competitor of the Gizmo Division, has accused Wright of engaging in unfair competitive practices. Alpha alleges that Wright is trying to drive out competition by having the Gizmo Division sell product for below-market prices while having the monopoly Widget Division charge higher prices to compensate.

As proof that Gizmo is charging below-market prices, Alpha presents you with the following:

- Alpha earned a profit margin of 20 percent on revenues, whereas the Gizmo Division earned a profit of 10 percent for the same period. Alpha is involved in manufacturing, processing, and retailing gizmos. Alpha is a fairly new, growth-stage company.
- Another competitor, Beta Inc., earned a profit margin of 25 percent as compared to 10 percent earned by the Gizmo Division. Beta is involved in manufacturing and retailing gizmos, but not in processing. Beta's gizmos are targeted to a specialty market, whereas Wright's gizmos are targeted to a mass market.
- Yet another competitor, Ceta Inc., earned a profit margin of 15 percent as compared to the Gizmo Division's 10 percent. Ceta is a retailer of gizmos and is a mature company. Its gizmos are targeted to a mass market.

In response the above, Ms. Christine, president of Wright, has stated that "it is simply impossible to compare the performance of our Gizmo Division with that of our competitors. To begin with, they aren't even in the same value chain. In addition, who knows if each company uses the same accounting policies? There are so many other reasons why we just can't make effective comparisons!"

Alpha also accuses Wright of underallocating costs to the Gizmo Division (in order to justify lower selling prices) and overallocating costs to the Widget Division (in order to justify higher selling prices).

Specifically, you learn that variable overhead costs are allocated to each division based on a proportion of total sales dollars earned by each respective division. Variable overhead includes such items as supervisory costs, quality control, machine setups, and maintenance. Meanwhile, fixed overhead costs are allocated based on the square footage occupied by the Widget and Gizmo Divisions in the common factory where they are located. Fixed overhead consists primarily of rent, hydro, heat, and water.

Required

1. Do you agree with the analysis presented by Alpha regarding the profit margins generated by the Gizmo Division versus the profit margins generated by competitors? Or do you agree with the claim made by Wright's president that comparisons are "impossible"? Explain, making any assumptions you consider necessary and identifying any issues you have with the information presented.

2. Do you have any issues with the allocation of variable and fixed overhead at Wright? What alternatives might you recommend, and which specific managerial decisions would this enhance or impede?

BRUNO'S RESTAURANT

Prem Lobo

Bruno Parmigiano is the owner and master chef of Bruno's Restaurant, which specializes in fine Italian cuisine. Recently, Bruno applied to have the interior of his restaurant remodelled on TV as part of the popular reality show, "The Re-Decorating Challenge." During the show, a celebrity interior designer selects a home or business, and with a team of assistants completely remodels the interior. Sadly, during the taping of the show, the celebrity designer, Frida Matisse, got a little carried away. A fire broke out, and Bruno's Restaurant was completely destroyed.

Bruno was devastated and is now suing Frida and her production company for the loss of his restaurant. As part of his lawsuit, he has hired an accountant to calculate the amount of his financial loss (see Exhibit 2). The calculation is basically meant to represent the future cash flow that the restaurant has lost as a result of the fire.

Frida has reviewed Bruno's loss calculation and has concerns that it does not reflect reality and that it overstates the loss. As she points out: "Bruno has basically calculated his loss based on foregone gross margin. I think his loss should be based on net income, which is a much lower figure. I don't even know if I agree with his calculation of gross margin anyhow! I guess what I am saying is that I really don't believe that all of the costs and revenues included in Bruno's loss calculation are relevant."

Frida has hired you to help her analyse the loss calculation. She has provided you with financial statements for the restaurant's operations prior to the fire (see Exhibit 1).

Required

Analyze and critique the loss calculation prepared by Bruno, using the information given. Prepare a revised calculation of loss based on your analysis. Be sure to address Frida's concerns. Clearly state any assumptions that you are making. Also, state any additional information you would like to have in order to finalize your analysis. **Hint:** Define "relevant," assess which costs are relevant, and analyze how costs may have changed as a result of the fire.

EXHIBIT 1: Financial Statements for Bruno's Restaurant

Year Ended December 31, 2006

Revenue	Note <1>	$600,000	
Cost of meals	Note <2>	250,000	
Gross margin		$350,000	58%

Operating Expenses

Depreciation		50,000	8%
Advertising	Note <3>	20,000	3
Management salaries	Note <4>	100,000	17
General and admin	Note <5>	50,000	8
Insurance		5,000	1
Property taxes		25,000	4
Rent	Note <6>	50,000	8
Total expenses		300,000	50%
Net income		**$50,000**	**8%**

Note <1> In 2006, revenues averaged $30 per meal for 20,000 meals served. Revenue per meal tends to fluctuate year by year based on consumer trends and tastes. Revenues per meal were $25 in 2003, $28 in 2004, and $27 in 2005.

Note <2> Cost of meals was $12.50 per meal and comprised the following:

Food ingredients	$5.00
Wages to kitchen staff	$4.00
Fixed restaurant overhead	$3.50
	$12.50

Note <3> Bruno has always regarded advertising as "essential" and as a "committed cost" each year. Since advertising was mainly in local newspapers and magazines, no binding contracts were signed between Bruno and the chosen newspapers and magazines.

Note <4> Management salaries were paid to Bruno.

Note <5> General and administrative expenses comprised the following:

$30,000 – Admin salaries for part-time bookkeepers and office help.

$10,000 – Water cooler rental fee for 2006. Bruno signed a water cooler rental contract, which had one year remaining at December 2006.

$10,000 – Tennis lessons for Bruno's wife.

Note <6> Rent for the restaurant location. Bruno has a 5-year rental agreement for his present location. The landlord is his father-in-law.

EXHIBIT 2: Calculation of Economic Loss to Bruno's Restaurant as a Result of the Fire, as Prepared by Bruno's Accountant

Foregone gross margin per year (as per financial statements)		$350,000
Opportunity cost	Note <1>	$50,000
Costs of lawsuit	Note <2>	$75,000
Foregone cash flow per year		**$475,000**
Number of years		10
Total foregone cash flow		$4,750,000
Emotional grief and suffering	Note <3>	500,000
Total economic loss to Bruno		**$5,250,000**

Note <1> Bruno had been thinking about renting out space in his restaurant to a group of musicians, who planned to serenade diners. As a result of the fire, Bruno was unable to proceed with his plans. The $50,000 represents the foregone rental fee per year.

Although Bruno had not actually spoken to the musicians and no arrangements existed to rent out the space, we believe the foregone rental amount of $50,000 to be reasonable based on the rental fees paid by musicians for rock concerts at local concert venues.

Note <2> The lawyer for Bruno estimates that by the time the lawsuit between Bruno and Frida is done, the total cost to Bruno will be $75,000.

Note <3> Bruno has experienced great emotional grief, suffering, and public embarrassment as a result of watching his restaurant burnt to a crisp on television.

GREAT CANADIAN ROCK TOURS

Alan J. Richardson

Great Canadian Rock Tours organizes bus charters to concerts and sports events. It focuses on attracting customers in small to medium-sized urban centres within a three-hour drive of large centres providing major concert and sports attractions. Basically, it provides two services: first, it provides transportation services, which allow customers to enjoy themselves without worrying about how they will get home after the event; and second, it acts as a speculator, buying tickets for events in bulk and then reselling them as part of its tour packages, often at a discount from the price charged by direct sales outlets. Since its sales of transportation services are dependent on its sales of event tickets, Great Canadian focuses its overall performance measurement system on ticket sales (transportation services are expected to minimize costs, but the firm's success depends on promoting the right events and selling a profitable mix of tickets).

For each event the company buys seats at a range of prices based on its estimate of the distribution of demand. For a recent event, a reunion tour of a 1970s heavy metal band, the company anticipated selling 200 tickets: 100 in the $30 seats, 60 in the $60 seats, and 40 in the $90 seats. The company buys the tickets from the concert promoters at $5 per ticket plus 40 percent of face value (i.e., $30 tickets are purchased for $5 + 0.4($30) = $17); those tickets are then non-refundable. Had it sold all of the tickets, the company would have accounted for 5 percent of the total seats available at the concert.

Unfortunately, an incident at a previous concert — the band mocked the fans' willingness to pay for nostalgia — reduced interest in this concert. Great Canadian was able to sell only 60 tickets in the $30 seats, and 15 in the $60 seats; however, a group of diehard fans bought 30 in the $90 seats. At the concert, a count of those in attendance indicated that only 62.5 percent of the seats had been sold, although a sell-out had been expected.

Great Canadian wants to learn from this experience. It believes that variance analysis should be able to provide insights into the economic consequences of these events, as well as suggest strategies for ensuring the profitability of such ventures.

Required

1. Use variance analysis to break down the consequences of the events described. Briefly explain each of the variances calculated. Indicate any design choices that you have made in selecting and calculating variances.
2. Based on the variance analysis, what changes in operating procedures would you recommend to Great Canadian Rock Tours?

SUMMER DREAMING FROZEN TREAT COMPANY: BUDGETING

Alan J. Richardson

The Summer Dreaming Frozen Treat Company is preparing for another year of selling frozen treats from pedal-powered carts throughout the city. To plan its activities, the company wants to prepare a budget for April and May that will show it the best results it can expect. It has provided you with data (see Exhibit 1) that you can assume represent reasonable estimates based on past experience.

EXHIBIT 1: Predicted Monthly Demand for Frozen Treats

April	May	June	July	August	September	Total
1,000	2,000	3,000	5,000	5,000	2,000	18,000

Sales are assumed to be equally distributed within each month.

The company can run advertisements in a local shopper's newspaper alongside announcements of major events during the summer at a cost of $20 per month (payable in advance). The company estimates that these ads would increase demand by about 15 percent.

EXHIBIT 2: Predicted Costs and Revenues

- Sales price for all frozen treats will be $0.80. All sales will be cash.
- Cost of goods sold will be $0.40 per frozen treat, on account payable one month after delivery. All orders must be placed at the beginning of the month; frozen treats are sold in cases of 144 treats per case. Same-day delivery is guaranteed.
- Warehouse space rental (for storage of frozen goods and security of carts after hours) is $100 per month, on a six-month contract, payable monthly in advance.
- Cart rental is $50 per month in advance. Carts are rented as needed on one-month contracts.
- Cyclist/salespeople wages are $200 per month, payable in arrears. Cyclists must be hired for the whole month. It has been the company's experience that one cyclist can sell 800 frozen treats per month.

EXHIBIT 3: Other Information

- Money can be borrowed or repaid in multiples of $500 at 1% interest per month. Interest is paid monthly on the first day of the month, repayments on the last day of the month.
- The company hopes to end the year with no inventory, since the goods are perishable. (There is no beginning inventory.)
- Income taxes and other incidental charges are ignored.

Required

Identify the operational choices that the company faces and provide recommendations — justified with calculations where appropriate — for how the business should proceed.

C H A P T E R   5

ADVANCED CASES

The advanced cases in this chapter provide slightly more complex situations. These cases provide more information about the situation facing the organization. The more complex the case, the more important it becomes to systematically use the case analysis process described in Chapter 2. This process will ensure that you have identified all of the issues in the case, understood the objectives and constraints facing the decision maker, generated a reasonable range of alternatives, considered the consequences of each alternative from the perspective of the decision maker, and, finally, presented a well reasoned and justifiable recommendation. You may find it helpful to reread Chapter 2 and review the example provided in Chapter 3 before proceeding with the cases in this chapter.

ADVENTURE CLOTHING: MAKE OR BUY

Charles Plant

Adventure Clothing has operated a direct-mail clothing business specializing in outdoor adventure clothing for more than 15 years. In the past five years it has increasingly been turning to the Internet to drive sales volume and so has been relying less on catalogues for customer interaction. However, it still produces a large number of catalogues on an annual basis, and it expects to produce between 400,000 and 600,000 catalogues a year for the next five years. The cost of catalogues is equal to about 8 percent of total catalogue sales.

These catalogues are produced in three separate waves, with one catalogue in each of November, March, and July. Because of the product emphasis in each of the catalogues, the November and March catalogues have equal distribution and the July catalogue is sent out at half the volume of either of the other two. The president of Adventure, Jon Herberman, has noted that the timing of catalogue delivery is very important; any slippage in delivery has the potential to ruin a season of sales.

The firm has operated its own printing facility since inception and has the capacity to produce 100,000 catalogues in any given month without any overtime, using its internal labour force. These people, who can produce 1,000 catalogues in 22 hours, are paid $15 per hour for regular time and time-and-a-half for any overtime. Unfortunately, as the catalogues are always ready for printing exactly one month ahead of time, there usually is a lot of overtime involved in the printing. The material costs for the catalogues are $0.16 per unit. Variable overhead is equal to 75 percent of labour costs; fixed overhead runs to $175,000 per year.

The firm has recently been considering outsourcing the catalogue production to two different firms. The first firm, Don's Printing, has proposed that it handle any amount of printing up to 400,000 catalogues a year for $1.15 per catalogue; after that, the price would decline 5 cents per 50,000 more produced until it hit a price of $0.95 at a volume of 600,000. If Adventure were to elect this or any other option, it could save half its fixed overhead, but only if it outsourced all the production. Don's Printing is noted for its quality, which is in fact superior to that of Adventure's in-house production, but it also has a reputation for being difficult to work with.

The second firm, Dave's Publishing, has proposed a slightly different deal: a fixed price per year of $300,000, plus $0.60 per catalogue at a volume of 400,000. After that the price would decline 5 cents per 50,000 more produced until it hit a price of $0.40 at a volume of 600,000. Dave's has a good reputation in other markets but has no reputation in this market, as it has just opened a local plant.

Required

Provide a report indicating what course of action the firm should take.

BROKEN ISLAND KAYAKS: SPECIAL PRICING

Charles Plant

Broken Island Kayaks had been manufacturing a premium line of sea kayaks for the past ten years. These kayaks are marketed throughout North America in specialty stores and are among the highest quality and highest priced kayaks on the market. About 85 percent of this firm's sales are in the United States, the remainder in Canada. The company is proud of its kayaks, which every year win industry-wide design and development awards. It makes six different models, which it sells to stores at an average price of $1,900. The average retail selling price of a Broken Island kayak is $2,850.

Unfortunately, because of the weak growth of the sport, the market for high-end kayaks has been declining for several years. Kayaks tend to last a long time, and the high-end market is saturated. As a consequence, annual demand for Broken Island kayaks has peaked recently at 740 units and is forecast to remain at that level over the next three years. The company had not anticipated the flat growth in demand, and recently expanded its facilities. It now has the capacity to produce 1,100 kayaks annually. The company's income statement for the previous year, in which it sold 740 kayaks, is provided in Exhibit 1.

EXHIBIT 1: Broken Island: Most Recent Income Statement

Revenue	$1,406,000
Material	160,000
Labour	320,000
Fixed overhead	350,000
Variable overhead	60,000
Cost of goods sold	890,000
Marketing	260,000
Commissions	140,000
Administration	135,000
Expenses	535,000
Loss	**$19,000**

Sea to Sky Co-op is a Canadian outdoor cooperative retail chain with stores in seven Canadian cities. It has recently approached Broken Island Kayaks and requested that the company private-label one of its models for sale by Sea to Sky. The retailer has offered a long-term contract to purchase 300 kayaks annually for the next three years at a price of $1,100 per kayak. It is not willing to pay a higher price because it plans to retail the kayak at only $1,695. Because this sale would involve a private label for an existing model, the company would have no new-product development costs for this order. Furthermore, it would not have to pay its regular commission rate of 10 percent, as the order was not brought in by the sales force.

Susan Calverley, the president of Broken Island Kayaks, is interested in Sea to Sky's offer even though the price is well below Broken Island's normal price. Her one concern is that the company may see a decline in sales with existing retailers, in that some customers will comparison shop and find the same-quality kayak available at a lower price in Sea to Sky stores. She has turned to you, a well-respected local consultant, for help in deciding what to do.

Required

Prepare a report to Ms. Calverley with your recommendations.

DRITEST CLOTHING: COMPENSATION

Charles Plant

DriTest Clothing is a Canadian company whose common shares are traded on the stock exchange. For the past fifteen years it had been steadily penetrating the market for technical clothing for active sports. It has created three divisions, each oriented around a group of sports. The Ski and Snowboard Division makes long underwear and a variety of microfibre layers designed for warmth and for absorbing sweat. The Running and Hiking Division makes shorts, tights, and polypropylene tops that feature flexible movement and rapid drying. The Yoga and Pilates Division is more fashion- and fit-oriented but maintains a high degree of functionality. Consumers' tastes and interests are changing, and the company has been seeing a movement in revenue away from colder sports toward warmer ones, as well as a movement from outdoor to indoor activities.

Lately the company has been experiencing weak profits, lack of sales growth, poor ROI, and a reduced stock price. To improve the company's operating results, the president, Brynn Winegard, has decided to implement a new bonus plan for each of her three divisional managers. He has a maximum of $150,000 to put into the plan, and she has asked you, the CFO of DriTest, for advice on how best to allocate this money among the divisional managers. Brynn also wants your advice on how to design this new bonus plan for the three divisional managers.

You have pulled together income statements, and other relevant data for the three divisions for the 2004 fiscal year (see Exhibit 1).

Required

Write a report to Brynn recommending a course of action for DriTest.

EXHIBIT 1: Dritest Financial Data ($000s)

	Ski and Snowboard	Running and Hiking	Yoga and Pilates
Net sales revenue	$12,700	$8,760	$5,310
Cost of sales	5,715	3,504	1,859
Gross margin	6,985	5,256	3,451
Operating expenses			
Personnel expenses	1,652	875	842
Allocated rent	350	350	350
Sales commissions	762	438	372
Allocated product development	185	185	185
Allocated advertising	1,800	1,800	1,800
General office	135	104	98
Allocated head office costs	267	267	267
Allocated interest	592	480	311
Total operating expenses	5,743	4,499	4,225
Net income (loss)	1,242	757	(774)
Square footage used	8,750	12,650	3,600
Revenue growth	−2%	7%	13%
Profit growth	−5%	2%	15%
Divisional investment			
Accounts receivable	$2,117	$973	$443
Inventories	953	876	531
Net plant fixed assets (net of liabilities)	875	1,350	1,100
Total	3,945	3,199	2,074

FEDORKIW DERAILLEUR: SPECIAL PRICING

Charles Plant

Fedorkiw Derailleur manufactures a technically superior line of bicycle derailleurs (which are the mechanisms for changing gears on mountain bikes). Its product is marketed to companies that assemble mountain bikes from components made by many manufacturers. These assemblers then market the finished bikes through retailers. The quality of a bike is determined by the quality of the components used in assembly. Fedorkiw is proud of the quality of its derailleurs. Because of this product's technical superiority and high price, it is used on only the finest mountain bikes sold. Fedorkiw makes three different models of derailleurs, which it sells to assemblers at an average price of $250.

The growing popularity of mountain bike racing has been driving up demand for high-end components, including derailleurs. The previous year, the company sold 5,600 derailleurs, and it has the capacity to produce only another 1,500. Because the market is growing, Fedorkiw expects an increase in sales next year, but it does not know how great the increase will be.

Revenue	$1,400,000
Material	160,000
Labour	320,000
Fixed overhead	350,000
Variable overhead	60,000
Cost of goods sold	890,000
Marketing	260,000
Commissions	140,000
Administration	135,000
Expenses	535,000
Loss	**$25,000**

The company's president is Terry Fedorkiw. Two different bike assemblers have recently approached him with requests that he supply derailleurs for their bikes. Neither of these companies has been a customer before. Lyuba Cycles is a Russian mountain bike firm that wants to buy 1,000 derailleurs at an average price of $125. The derailleurs would be used on high-end mountain bikes for exclusive sale in Russia, a market in which Fedorkiw has no existing sales. Chislett Cycles wants Terry to supply it with 1,000 derailleurs, which it would use for mid-range mountain bikes to be sold in North America. Chislett is offering to buy the product at an average price of $150. These offers are tempting, as the company would face no new marketing, commission, or administration costs as a result of the orders.

Terry Fedorkiw is interested in these offers, even though the price would be well below normal price. His one concern with Chislett's offer is that the company might see a decline in sales with existing assemblers, since he would be putting his product on a mid-range bike, with potential harm to his carefully crafted image for high-end derailleurs. Terry has turned to you, a well-respected local consultant, for help in deciding what to do.

Required

Prepare a report to Terry Fedorkiw with your recommendations.

GOODMAN BARNES & KIM: COMPENSATION

Charles Plant

Goodman Barnes & Kim was created from the merger of three companies ten years ago. Goodman was the king of the toilet industry in Canada; Barnes specialized in sinks; Kim was dominant in the bathtub area. The fastest growing area of the business is sinks, which grew revenue by 20 percent in 2005. Toilets grew 10 percent that year, whereas bathtubs fell by 5 percent. The company's strategy had been to maximize annual profits. It is owned by the descendants of the founders, who rely on high annual dividends to support their respective lifestyles.

The following is the 2005 financial statement for the company.

Revenue	$30,000,000
Cost of goods sold	20,920,000
Research and development	2,000,000
Sales and marketing	2,850,000
Administration (including bonus)	1,925,000
Profit	2,305,000

In 2005, the three products manufactured by the plant had revenues and costs as follows:

Per unit	Toilets	Sinks	Bathtubs
Units sold	26,000	12,000	20,000
Selling price	400	300	800
Material cost	120	75	220
Labour cost	70	650	200
Maintenance hours	800	400	1,500
Machine hours	500	300	1,600

Variable overhead included both maintenance costs and machine operating costs. Total maintenance costs were $1,200,000, and machine operating costs were $1,750,000. Fixed overhead was $2,950,000 and was allocated according to the amount of variable overhead. Research and development focused entirely on new products, not on line extensions or product improvements. Administration and sales and marketing were each dependent on the dollar value of sales in any area.

The company's total capital employed was $33 million, of which $15 million was for toilets, $6 million for sinks, and $12 million for bathtubs. Equity equalled 40 percent of capital employed and cost 18 percent. Debt represented the other 60 percent of capital and cost 5 percent. The president made all of the decisions regarding capital investments.

The president, Bettina Levina, has five managers reporting directly to her, one for each of the product lines, another for research, and another for administration. Each product line manager is responsible for all sales and costs for the product. These product managers all work closely together. Maintaining a positive working environment is important to Bettina.

The three product line managers have always been paid generous base salaries, and in 2005 each was also paid a bonus of $85,000. However, for 2006 it will not be possible to increase their bonuses (which in 2005 totalled $255,000). As the company has not yet prepared a budget for 2006, Bettina needs to use the 2005 numbers to develop a new bonus structure.

The company is planning to go public in one year, and Bettina wants to revise the bonus structure in anticipation of that event. She has heard that the stock market rewards return on investment and growth in revenue, and she isn't sure whether she should factor this into her plan for bonuses.

Required

Write a report recommending a course of action for Goodman Barnes & Kim.

MACLEISH NURSERIES: BUDGETING

Charles Plant

MacLeish Nurseries wholesales non-seasonal plants. Sales for the previous three quarters ending September 31, 2004, were poor because of the cold spring and summer. The plants could be sold at two times cost to other wholesalers, but the company had 3.5 million plants that it could not sell in the following quarter. Also, the firm's banker is asking for its loan to be paid down to below $500,000 and the manager, Kathleen Biro, is worried about whether she will receive her new share options, which will be released if revenue meets or exceeds this year's budget of $18 million. For some time the company's owners have been considering selling the business; they are now very interested in improving profits in order to enhance the sales price.

Below is the 2004 financial statement for MacLeish for the first three quarters ($000s).

	Q1	Q2	Q3
Sales revenue	$2,000	$4,000	$5,000
Expenses			
Cost of goods sold	500	1000	1,250
Fixed salaries	800	800	800
Variable salaries	300	600	750
Rent	200	200	200
General	300	500	600
Advertising	400	800	1,000
Total expenses	2,500	3,900	4,600
Profit	−500	100	400
Units sold (000)	1,000	2,000	2,500
Bank loan	1,500	1,400	1,000

Sales in the fourth quarter are normally equal to sales in the third quarter, and all indications are that this will be the case for this year as well.

The company has noticed that its results depend heavily on two factors: advertising and price. Over time, it has noticed that any change in advertising from seasonal levels results in a 2.5-to-1 change in sales. In other words, a $1 change in advertising results in a $2.50 change in sales from otherwise normal seasonal levels. In terms of pricing, a 2 percent decrease in the retail price of plants results in a 4 percent increase in sales volume. Similarly, a 2 percent increase in the price results in a 4 percent decrease in sales volume.

Required

Write a report recommending a course of action for MacLeish Nurseries.

MERIDIAN TELESCOPES: PRODUCTION PLANNING

Charles Plant

Meridian has been manufacturing fine telescopes for 80 years. It has developed a well-earned reputation for quality craftsmanship. It makes two lines of telescopes in its 200,000-square-foot facility. The older line, for which there is steady demand and on which Meridian's strong reputation is based, consists of small professional scopes. Based on the success of this original line, the company introduced a second line of amateur telescopes for people who wanted a telescope with the Meridian brand but who could not afford the high retail prices.

The company now hopes to bring out a line of binoculars and estimates that it could sell between 50,000 and 100,000 of them in the first year at a price of $300. It estimates that if it manufactured these in-house, labour would cost $45 per unit, material would cost $60 per unit, and variable overhead would be 50 percent of labour costs. Manufacturing would take one square foot of space per binocular manufactured in the year. Alternatively, the firm could outsource the manufacturing of the binoculars for $175 per unit. The addition of this line, because it would complement other lines, would add no additional general and administrative costs. However, sales and marketing would be 10 percent of revenue.

Cathy Kain is the president of Meridian. She is trying to make some production planning decisions. The company has fully utilized its present manufacturing plant, and any new plant would not be ready for three years. She has concerns about quality issues connected with outsourcing. Even so, she has obtained quotations for outsourcing the two lines of telescopes, the professional model at a cost of $9,000 per unit and the amateur model at a cost of $2,250 per unit. In terms of other expenses connected with the option to outsource, Cathy has determined that general administrative costs would not change but that sales and marketing costs would fluctuate with the volume of product sold.

On the next page is a summary of the firm's costs for telescopes.

Required

Write a report recommending a course of action for Meridian.

	Pro quality	Amateur
Units produced and sold	500	9,000
Unit selling price	$12,000	$3,000
Facility square footage used	50,000	150,000
Costs per unit		
Labour	$5,500	$500
Material	2,000	500
Variable overhead	2,750	250
Fixed overhead	1,375	125
	11,625	1,375
Outsource cost	9,000	2,250
Operating costs		
Sales and marketing	900,000	2,700,000
General administrative costs	250,000	1,000,000

NAYLOR SECURITY INC.: PRODUCTION PLANNING

Charles Plant

For seven years, Naylor Security had been developing security products such as palmprint and fingerprint entry pads as well as voice print analysis equipment. It has enjoyed considerable success for most of that time. Its security devices are being used to control access to businesses, labs, factories, and high-security installations around the world. The company operates in North America through its Toronto office and in Asia through its Beijing facility. The manufacturing of Naylor products is done in both locations. However, U.S. government purchasers (who account for half the Toronto plant's revenue) typically are hesitant to buy non–NAFTA-produced security devices. The security sector has become highly competitive in recent years, and while there are plenty of potential new customers, there are also plenty of new competitors. The company had usually enjoyed strong profits; but those profits have declined in the past year.

The company makes three products: a fingerprint analyzer, a palmprint analyzer, and a voiceprint analyzer. All three products can be made in either Toronto or Beijing. At present, the Toronto plant manufactures all three products, although it could choose to buy them from Beijing. The Toronto plant's sales volumes and production data on a monthly basis are as follows:

	Palmprint	Fingerprint	Voiceprint
Units produced	550	1,050	900
Unit selling price	695	450	850
Material cost	100	175	125
Labour cost	135	150	75
Cost if Naylor buys from Beijing plant	495	425	195

Other facts are as follows:

- Labour costs are $15 per hour.
- Variable overhead cost is 60 percent of the amount spent for labour on average for any product manufactured.
- Fixed overhead costs of $500,000 per month cannot be eliminated for eight years.
- The firm allocates fixed overhead to each product as a percentage of revenue for that product.
- Research and development of new products is $100,000 per month.
- Sales commissions are paid at a rate of 5 percent of revenue.
- Selling, general, and administration (SG&A) cost is $150,000 per month.

The firm's R&D department has recently developed a retinal scanner that is expected to be in high demand. Initial forecasts for the next year are for a monthly demand of between 150 and 300 units. These scanners are expected to sell for $925 per unit, with material costs of $210 and labour of $165. The Beijing plant could supply to Toronto at a cost of $650 per unit. R&D and SG&A were not expected to increase as a result of the new product's introduction.

The Toronto plant has labour capacity of only 20,000 hours per month, so there is some question as to whether the new product should be produced in Toronto or Beijing. Also, the Toronto plant plans to evaluate its production mix to determine whether it should be outsourcing any other products to Beijing or discontinuing some products entirely.

Required

Prepare a report recommending the course of action the company should take.

OAK RIDGES FURNITURE: COMPENSATION

Charles Plant

Oak Ridges Furniture has been manufacturing and selling dining room tables and chairs since the late 1970s. Business has been excellent lately, and the firm has been recording very healthy profits. In large part, the healthy profits are due to the efforts of the manufacturing personnel, whose innovative approaches to manufacturing have greatly reduced the amount of time required to produce the company's furniture.

Below is the 2003 financial statement for the company.

Revenue	$21,250,000
Cost of goods sold	11,675,000
Sales and marketing	1,850,000
Administration	925,000
Profit	6,800,000

The two product lines manufactured by the plant had revenues and costs as follows:

Per unit	Tables	Chairs
Units sold	40,000	150,000
Selling price	250	75
Material cost	25	10
Labour cost	80	15
Manufacturing personnel	80	45

Variable overhead was equal to 50 percent of labour costs. Fixed overhead cost a total of $1,000,000 and was applied by the company to each division on a ratio of revenue. Administration and sales and marketing were each dependent on the dollar value of sales in any area.

The company president, Rick Hay, wants to change the compensation package for all of his manufacturing personnel because of the excellent job they have been doing in bringing down manufacturing costs. He has no set amount in mind. His objective is to ensure that the company has a 25 percent profit level before tax, but he is not sure how he should calculate this extra compensation.

Required

Write a report recommending a course of action for Oak Ridges Furniture.

ROTHWELL METAL STAMPING: RETURN ON INVESTMENT

Charles Plant

Rothwell Metal Stamping manufactures small, high-precision metal parts for a variety of industrial needs. The company is organized with three divisions, each division serving a unique market sector.

Over the past several years the company has found it more and more difficult to raise capital as investors have been looking for more modern industries in which they think they can obtain a better return. In the upcoming year the company has requests for funding from divisions totalling $13 million. The Automotive Division is looking for $3 million for a variety of projects; the Appliances Division is seeking $6 million for several new initiatives in China; and the Leisure Products Division is asking for $4 million for a variety of things. David Chan, the president of Rothwell, knows that each division has padded its request and could actually benefit from any amount of money. But in total, he has only $5 million of funding available to meet their requests.

The three divisions have each presented very similar business cases showing almost identical healthy future returns from these investments; as a consequence, David is having difficulty deciding how to allocate the investment funds. He has decided that the best way to allocate the funds would be to use measures of past performance and then to award the funds to the division(s) with the best record(s) of providing returns to the company. He is unsure, though, whether he should use return on investment, residual income, or economic value added to measure the effectiveness of his divisions. The results for the company are shown on the next page.

Required

Recommend the appropriate course of action for David Chan.

	Automotive Division	Appliance Division	Leisure Products Division
Sales revenue	$4,200	$6,300	$3,200
Expenses			
Direct material and labour	1,064	1,798	995
Supplies	44	133	35
Maintenance and repairs	200	150	60
Plant depreciation	120	90	180
Administration	120	90	180
Total expenses	1,548	2,261	1,450
Divisional margin	2,652	4,039	1,750
Interest charge	375	680	204
Allocated corporate fixed costs	613	920	467
Divisional profits	$1,664	$2,439	$1,079

	Automotive Division	Appliance Division	Leisure Products Division
Divisional investment			
Accounts receivable	$550	$895	$285
Inventories	350	250	650
Net plant fixed assets	2,850	5,650	1,100
Total	$3,750	$6,795	$2,035

	Automotive Division	Appliance Division	Leisure Products Division
Capital requested	3,000	6,000	4,000
Rate on marginal debt	6%	6%	6%
Rate on marginal equity	17%	17%	17%
Debt % capital	50%	50%	50%

SHEPARD POLES: BUDGETING

Charles Plant

Shepard Poles has been manufacturing and selling specialized poles for the past ten years. The company is organized around three different lines: hiking poles, downhill ski poles, and cross-country ski poles. The three products manufactured by the company had revenues and costs as follows:

Per unit	Cross-country	Hiking	Downhill
Units sold	100,000	150,000	200,000
Selling price/unit	31	52	40
Material cost unit	11	5	4.5
Labour cost/unit	12	28	24

Variable overhead includes maintenance costs and machine costs and is equal to 20 percent of labour costs. Fixed overhead costs are $950,000 and are charged to products according to the amount of variable overhead. Other costs are as follows:

Research and development	350,000
Sales and marketing	1,850,000
Administration	925,000

R&D focuses entirely on new products, not on line extensions or product improvement. Administration and sales and marketing costs both depend on the dollar value of sales in any area. Unit sales are expected to increase overall by about 7 percent next year before any new strategic initiatives are implemented; all costs are rising by about 2 percent.

Each of the company's three vice presidents has suggested a strategic initiative to move the company forward in the next year. Each alternative is separate and distinct. Because of management time pressures, Shephard can implement only one of these alternatives next year. The three alternatives are as follows:

1. *Introduce a new product.* The company has been working for the past year on a new hiking pole that it had planned originally to launch in fiscal 2006. The one drawback to this option is that it would reduce demand for its existing hiking poles on a four-for-one basis — that is, the sale of four new poles would mean that one less old pole was sold. The costs to manufacture the new pole would be the same as for the old pole. Also, the new technology would allow the company to increase the price of its poles by $8 per unit. The company expects that it would be able to sell 55,000 poles in the first year after launch.

2. *Increase promotion.* The company could delay the launch of the new product until a later year and strengthen its promotion of existing products. The new promotion would cost $50,000 for a new marketing campaign and $65,000 for a new inside sales person. It is expected that this initiative would increase revenue between 20 and 30 percent in the first year; however, it would have no incremental effects in following years except for the fact that the company would be better known.

3. *Raise prices and cut costs.* Naturally, the VP Finance wants to raise prices and reduce costs. He thinks that prices could be increased by 2 percent with no drop-off in volume; also, that if prices were increased by 4 percent, volume might drop by 3 to 5 percent. He also thinks that costs could be cut by at least 1 percent across the board without much damage to the company. It might lose personnel, but the VP Finance thinks that that isn't very important as these people could be replaced.

Barb Shepard is hoping to sell the company soon and knows that buyers will be looking at three main factors in arriving at a purchase price for the company: the absolute level of profits, the rate of growth in profits, and future potential growth in the market. Also, she needs to reduce bank debt as soon as possible as she has reached the maximum allowable level of debt and every dollar of profits or losses goes directly to reduce or increase bank debt. She needs to come up with a budget and plan for the next year.

Required

Write a report recommending a course of action for Shepard Poles.

BOLAND ASSEMBLIES INC.: COMPENSATION

Charles Plant

Boland Assemblies has been manufacturing industrial cabinets for more than 20 years and has enjoyed considerable success for most of that time. Unfortunately, the business has become highly competitive recently and new customers have become hard to find. The company long experienced strong profits, but profits have turned into losses in recent years and the company has been finding it difficult to keep employees on board, as there are strong pressures on profits. Because of declining revenue, the company has plenty of capacity to bring on new business.

Of particular concern to Chris Boland, the president and owner of Boland Assemblies, is the turnover in salespeople. Each of the 10 salespeople is paid a base salary of about $24,000 per year, which is lower than the $48,000 industry standard. In addition, each receives a commission based on the profitability of orders he or she brings into the company. Expectations in the industry are for a total compensation package of $125,000. Paul Burk, the company's leading salesperson and a long-term employee, has just announced that he is about to land a new account. While he is excited about the potential of this new account, he is concerned that the customer will want a price far lower than what Boland customers usually pay.

This is a secretive industry, so Boland isn't worried about reducing prices for this one customer — he is confident that no other customers will find out. Furthermore, prices are not comparable between customers owing to the customized manufacturing processes employed for each cabinet. This new customer has also indicated that it will not be willing to negotiate price, design, manufacturing, or any feature of its proposal. This is a "take it or leave it" opportunity without any strategic issues or risks to the company.

Boland's most recent annual income statement is provided below. This year is expected to show similar results if the company doesn't get the new order.

Revenue	$10,600,000
Material	920,000
Labour	1,640,000
Fixed overhead	2,300,000
Variable overhead	920,000
Cost of goods sold	5,780,000
Marketing	2,520,000
Commissions	760,000
Administration	1,670,000
Expenses	4,950,000
Loss	$130,000

The new client is proposing to contract for $2.5 million of new cabinets in the coming year. Materials are expected to cost 25 percent of the revenue; labour to manufacture is expected to be 30 percent. Variable overhead tends to fluctuate with the amount of labour required for the job. Marketing costs would not increase as a result of the order, and neither would administration. To calculate commissions, Chris Boland subtracts actual material and labour from an order as well an estimate for overhead. For several years, based on calculations made by a consultant, he has been using 40 percent of revenue as an estimate for overhead. This approach results in an estimated gross profit for each order. Normally, commissions are then calculated at a rate of 20 percent of estimated gross profit.

Both Chris and Paul have concerns that the order won't bring in a profit. Even so, the company needs the revenue and so the order has been accepted. Paul is also concerned that the order will result in very little commission to him and is a bit discouraged about it, considering how hard he had to work to land the order and that this is going to be his only order for the year. For some time he has been thinking about leaving the firm and taking the opportunity with him to another manufacturer; but he also feels that he owes some allegiance to Boland Assemblies. He contends that given this new business potential, this would be a good time to work out a new method for calculating his commission. He would be happy to stay with the firm if a new deal could be worked out.

Required

Prepare a report recommending the course of action the company should take.

BLUE RIDGE ICE CREAM

Tony Dimnik

Racey Lee, the owner of Blue Ridge Ice Cream (BRIC), knew that Bart Uday, the manager of the Kingston store, would be unhappy with his bonus for May 2005. May had been very busy for the Kingston store, and although Bart had worked long and hard, his results were significantly below budget.

BRIC operates five ice cream stores in the Thousand Islands tourist region of eastern Ontario. The stores are open four months each year, from May to August. Every April, Racey finalizes budgets for each of the stores. Table 1 shows the May 2005 budget for the Kingston store. Sales volume, which is expressed in terms of "number of ice cream cones," is based on average monthly sales for each store in past years. The selling price for each ice cream cone is set at $2.00. The cost of cones and ice cream is negotiated with suppliers for the four-month period, and the $1.25 budgeted cost is estimated using standard product mix and standard quantities, which include waste and spoilage. The rental expense in the budget is a fixed cost; the electricity expense is based on expected usage and the most recent hydro rates.

Each store has its own manager, usually a university student. Staff and managers were paid $10 per hour, but managers usually receive a bonus of 20 percent of the store's monthly profits. Racey exercises some discretion regarding the bonuses. For example, in 2004 the manager of the Gananoque store exceeded every one of his 2004 monthly profit targets because one of his competitors went out of business. Racey felt that the Gananoque manager's results were not the result of any special effort on his part, so she paid him a bonus of less than 20 percent. On the other hand, when the manager of the Brockville

TABLE 1: Budget and Actual Results for the Kingston Store, May 2005

	Budget	Actual
Forecast number of ice cream cones sold	31,000	
Actual number of ice cream cones sold		40,000
Revenues	62,000	80,000
COGS	38,750	60,000
Gross profit	23,250	20,000
Staff and manager wages	3,720	4,960
Rent	1,500	1,500
Electricity	1,700	2,000
Profit before tax	16,330	11,540
Taxes at 30%	4,899	3,462
Profit after tax	11,431	8,078
Normal bonus of 20%	2,286	1,616

store had two months of lower-than-expected profits in 2004 because of nearby road construction, Racey paid her a bonus based on budgeted profits, rather than the lower actual profits.

Each BRIC manager is responsible for hiring, training, organizing, and motivating staff. Managers affect profit in several ways:

- Volumes are highly dependent on customer waiting times. Every BRIC location has nearby competitors, and long line-ups prompt customers to go to the competition. Managers can reduce waiting times by scheduling extra staff during peak times.
- According to company policy, employees must weigh each cone to ensure a minimum quantity of ice cream. However, during busy times managers often let employees add extra ice cream to each cone so that they won't have to return to the ice cream tubs to top up cones that are too light.
- According to company policy, employees must scoop out all the ice cream in each tub. However, during busy times, managers often let employees throw out near-empty tubs and replace them with new ones to avoid the time-consuming task of digging out ice cream from the bottom of each tub.

Racey has tried to emphasize the importance of properly weighted cones and of using all the ice cream in tubs. The managers have replied that they need some flexibility to reduce waiting times and to avoid stressing out busy staff. In a preliminary discussion with Racey about the May results, Bart has openly disagreed with the policies: "We have to cut some corners when we're busy. It's more important to serve customers quickly than to fiddle with serving sizes and to have people sticking their heads into tubs to get out the last scoop." Racey has promised to reassess the policies and to analyze Bart's results for a meeting to be held on June 5.

In preparation for the meeting, Racey has conducted an analysis of sales data and temperatures from all five locations over the past five years. From this, she has learned that sales vary almost exactly 10 percent from budgeted amounts for each degree difference in a location's monthly mean temperature. For example, Kingston has a normal mean May temperature of 16°C, but May 2005 was much warmer than usual and had a mean temperature of 18°C. Racey expects that the sales volume in Kingston for May should have been about 20 percent higher than budgeted.

As Racey looks at the May financial statement for Kingston (see Table 1), she wonders whether she should adjust Bart's bonus from the normal 20 percent of profit.

Required

Assume the role of Racey Lee and prepare a memo for Bart explaining your analysis of the May results for Kingston, your bonus decision, and your views on the serving size and empty tub policies. Racey feels that it is important that Bart be able to understand her logic before the meeting so that he can prepare an appropriate response.

COMPWARE CANADA (A)[1]

Tony Dimnik

Sean McDonnell has been the manager of the Canadian subsidiary of Compware for only a few weeks. He is already asking questions about the financial information he is getting. Sean worked in the sales department of Compware Canada for six years before being promoted, and during those years he never thought much about financial details. As long as he met his sales targets and received his commissions, he saw no need to ask questions about the financial reports that were circulated throughout the company on a regular basis. But now that he has overall responsibility for operations, he is beginning to wonder about some of the numbers. They just don't make sense.

Compware Financial Summary for 2003

	Alpha	Beta	Ceta	Totals
Unit sales	500	1,000	2,000	3,500
Revenues	$50,000	$200,000	$600,000	$850,000
Direct costs	25,000	125,000	350,000	500,000
Indirect costs	17,647	70,588	211,765	300,000
Gross profit	7,353	4,412	38,235	50,000
Unit profit	$14.71	$4.41	$19.12	$14.29

This 2003 financial summary is a simplified version of the reports that Sean receives on a regular basis. The reports focus on the three different software solutions sold by Compware. The software is sold on a site-by-site basis. Thus "units" refers to the number of new site installations. The installation of the software requires some consultation with the customer, and this often necessitates some modifications to the software and to the customer's computer setup. The 2003 summary shows that all three products were marginally profitable that year.

To better understand his financials, Sean has plotted Compware revenues and profits over the past five years. While revenues have climbed steadily, profits have been erratic. Sean looks at the graphical representation of revenues and profits, shakes his head, and sighs: "I don't see any connection between profits and revenues. What's going on here?"

Sean is also concerned about the profitability of the five main customers serviced by Compware. He asks his controller, Sid Lee, to prepare a table showing profitability by customer. When Sid gives Sean the results of his analysis, Sean grimaces: "These profit numbers don't make sense. For example, I know that we spent an awful lot of time working with Wastern. Each of their branches calls us on an individual basis. We handled 85 orders from Wastern last year. On the other hand, Yavol had only 20 orders and their sales are higher. Yet their profits are lower. This doesn't make sense."

---

[1] The case is based on the experiences of several companies and represents actual business situations. However, similarities between the company and the people described in the case and actual companies and people are not intended.

FIGURE 1: Compware Revenues and Profits

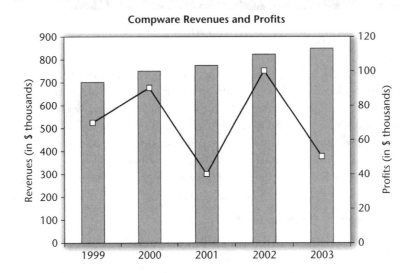

Customer Profitability Analysis

	Veso	Western	Xero	Yavol	Zed	Totals
Alpha units sold	200	150	100	50	0	500
Beta units sold	0	100	200	300	400	1,000
Ceta units sold	200	400	600	400	400	2,000
Orders	5	85	30	20	100	240
Revenues	$80,000	$155,000	$230,000	$185,000	$200,000	$850,000
Costs	$73,235	$144,706	$216,176	$175,294	$190,588	$800,000
Profit	**$6,765**	**$10,294**	**$13,824**	**$9,706**	**$9,412**	**$50,000**

"Hmmm," says Sid as she looks over the table. "Obviously, Yavol's product mix has a lower profit than that of Wastern. Yavol buys much more of the low-profit Beta. But I understand your point. Our system doesn't account for the effort involved in processing orders for different customers. Let's see what we might do about it."

With that, Sid proceeds to draw a diagram. "Look here," she says. "Our system is designed to give us the costs of each of our three products. We can directly trace more than half of our costs to the products. Our direct costs are $500,000 and most of that is what we pay to Compware U.S. Then we have a pool of costs of about $300,000 that are more difficult to trace to each product. We allocate these costs to products on the basis of revenue. For example, sales of Ceta represent more than half of our total revenues so more than half of indirect costs are allocated to Ceta. The way it works out is that the greater a product's revenue, the more indirect costs are allocated to it."

"Why do we do that?" asks Sean.

"Well, it's a simple and easy way to do it . . . and I guess it's fair. The more revenue a product generates the more costs it can bear."

FIGURE 2: Cost Diagram

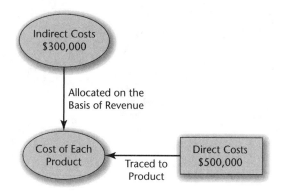

"Sid, those indirect costs are more than one-third of our total costs. We take the effort of tracking two-thirds of the costs. It just doesn't make sense to arbitrarily allocate the other third."

"No, I guess not," agrees Sid. "When our accounting staff implemented this system seven or eight years ago, indirect costs weren't that large. Now that they're 38 percent of our total costs we should take another look at how they're allocated."

"Great," says Sean. "Do that. And instead of calculating the cost on a product basis, do it on a customer basis. I think we could manage our costs and our profits much better if we had a better handle on who's really costing us what."

A few days later, Sid returns with some diagrams and tables. She starts off by showing Sean this diagram. "What I've done here is change the cost object from product to customer. We know which customer is buying which product, so the direct costs of the product are still direct costs of the customers. However, I've done a quick study of the indirect costs and found that about 70 percent of those indirect costs or $210,000 are due to order processing. When a customer calls us for an order, we have to set up a file, conduct an on-site consultation, prepare an installation plan, and so on. These costs are basically the same regardless of whether the order is for one unit or ten units and regardless of the product. We process about 240 orders per year so, on average, orders cost us $875 each."

"OK, I follow you so far," says Sean. "But I don't think that one order is the same as another. Sometimes all we have to do is to take down an order, but other times we have to do a lot of consultation and background work before we install anything."

"Sure," agreed Sid. "However, this is a first cut. We can refine it later. You can also see that I haven't analyzed the other $90,000 of indirect costs. I'm just allocating it to each customer on the basis of revenue. The more revenue a particular customer generates, the more of the $90,000 gets allocated to it. Here's a table that demonstrates the differences between the original and new costing systems for three hypothetical orders of Alpha. What the table says is that if a customer orders ten units of Alpha, under our current costing system, that order will show a profit of $147. Under the new costing system, a ten-unit order of Alpha will show a loss of $481."

FIGURE 3: Cost Diagram

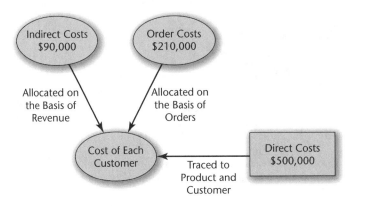

	Original Costing System			New Costing System		
Order size	1 unit	10 units	100 units	1 unit	10 units	100 units
Revenue	100	1,000	10,000	100	1,000	10,000
Direct cost	50	500	5,000	50	500	5,000
Indirect cost	35	353	3,530	11	106	1,060
Order processing cost	0	0	0	875	875	875
Total cost	85	853	8,530	936	1,481	6,935
Profit	**15**	**147**	**1,470**	**(836)**	**(481)**	**3,065**

"That makes sense," says Sean. "Whether we install one unit or one hundred units, the order processing costs would be in the same ballpark."

Comparing Profits Calculated by Original and New Systems on Orders of Alpha

	Veso	Western	Xero	Yavol	Zed	Totals
Revenues	80,000	155,000	230,000	185,000	200,000	850,000
Direct (product) costs	45,000	90,000	135,000	110,000	120,000	500,000
Order costs	4,375	74,375	26,250	17,500	87,500	210,000
Indirect costs	8,471	16,412	24,353	19,588	21,176	90,000
Total costs	57,846	180,787	185,603	147,088	228,676	800,000
"New" profit	**22,154**	**−25,787**	**44,397**	**37,912**	**−28,676**	**50,000**
"Original" profit	6,765	10,294	13,824	9,706	9,412	50,000

"Right. Now look what happens when we apply this thinking and recalculate the profits of each of our customers." Sid pulls out another table and hands it over to Sean. Sean pores over it for a minute and then looks up. "Are you sure you didn't make a mistake? What you're saying here is that Western and Zed are unprofitable — they're actually costing us money?"

FIGURE 4: Customer Profitability

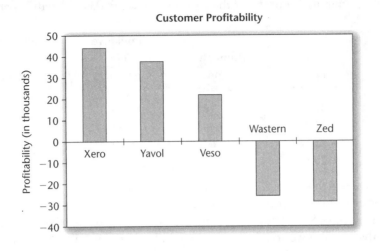

Customer Profitability

FIGURE 5: Identifying Profitable Customers

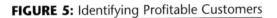

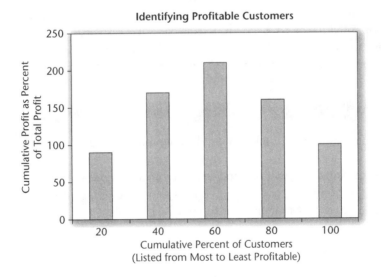

Identifying Profitable Customers

"I was as surprised as you are," replies Sid. "Take Zed for example. They made 100 orders last year — that's why they're a loss customer. I wondered why they were making so many orders so I asked around. Do you know that Zed has decentralized its operations and downsized its Information Systems Department? So one of the reasons why they're making so many orders is that each branch is acting on its own. But another reason is that with less IS support available, the Zed branches are using us as cheap consultants."

Sid continues: The final thing I did was plot a couple of graphs. The first one shows the profitability of each of our customers.

"To draw the second graph, I listed each of our customers in order of profitability and then plotted the cumulative profit of the customers against the cumulative percentage of customers."

Customers	Profit	Cumulative Profit	Cumulative % of Customers	Cumulative Profit as % of Total Profit
Xero	44,397	44,397	20	89
Yavol	37,912	82,309	40	165
Veso	22,154	104,463	60	209
Western	−25,787	78,676	80	157
Zed	−28,676	50,000	100	100

"If I'm reading this second graph right," says Sean, "you're telling me that if we dropped Wastern and Zed, our profits would double."

"Not quite," says Sid. "Some of the order processing costs are fixed so we'd have to do more analysis before we could say what would happen if we dropped customers."

"Thanks," says Sean. "I need some time to let this information sink in."

A few days later, Sean circulates the material that Sid has prepared and calls a meeting to discuss changing Compware's costing system. He approaches the meeting with some trepidation because Kris Apt, Compware's top salesperson, has served notice that he is vehemently opposed to the new system. Kris is currently responsible for the Western and Zed accounts and worked on the team that landed those accounts. He is paid a substantial commission on the revenues generated by the two accounts.

Required

1. Assume the role of Sean McDonnell. How would you "sell" the new system at the meeting?
2. How do you think Kris will respond to Sean's presentation?
3. How should Compware use the new information? Be prepared to suggest how customers and competitors might react to your suggestions.

COMPWARE CANADA (B)[2]

Tony Dimnik

At Sean's prompting, Compware Canada has adopted a new costing system that calculates costs on a customer-by-customer basis and that uses the number of orders as the key for allocating order-processing costs. The information from the new costing system has prompted two changes in the way Compware does business.

The first change has been to charge customers $875 for every order. Surprisingly, customers don't seem to resist this new charge. A typical customer response is surprise that Compware has not already been passing on order costs: "We knew you would eventually have to do it — we're doing it ourselves with our customers."

The second change has been to reduce the order processing costs themselves. In the past year, Compware has taken a number of steps that have reduced the cost of an order to about $740.

The 2004 financial results reflect the changes:

Compware Financial Summary for 2004

	Veso	Western	Xero	Yavol	Zed	Totals
Revenues	83,704	184,630	244,815	199,815	237,037	950,000
Direct (product) costs	45,000	90,000	135,000	110,000	120,000	500,000
Order costs	3,704	29,630	14,815	14,815	37,037	100,000
Indirect costs	13,216	29,152	38,655	31,550	37,427	150,000
Total costs	61,920	148,782	188,470	156,365	194,464	750,000
Profit	**21,784**	**35,848**	**56,345**	**43,450**	**42,573**	**200,000**
Number of orders	5	40	20	20	50	135

Sean is happy with the results — especially with the fourfold increase in profits over the previous year. At a meeting with Sid, the controller, he suggests that they now review the allocation of the remaining pool of indirect costs:

"I've been hearing lots of talk about introducing a new product to our current mix. I've kept in close touch with our customers and I really don't see the need for it — especially when we consider the costs of supporting a new product. For example, we have to maintain a complete set of documents for each product, and each product requires specialized training of current staff and hiring of new staff. I want our product mix to be up to date, but at the same time, I would like our costing system to reflect the cost of adding products. I think our salespeople are too quick to suggest new products as a solution to any problem. They get paid on commission, so it's not surprising that they only look at

---

[2] The case is based on the experiences of several companies and represents actual business situations. However, similarities between the company and the people described in the case and actual companies and people are not intended.

FIGURE 6: Cost Diagram

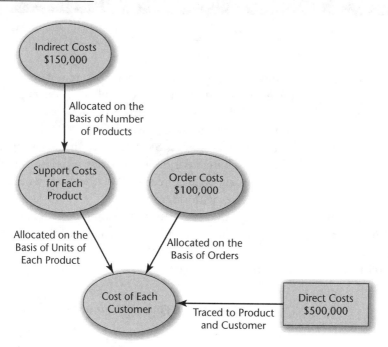

revenues and not at costs. If we add a new product, our revenues might increase and it may mean a few more dollars of commissions in the salespeople's pockets, but what will happen to the bottom line?"

Sean continues: "And since I'm on the topic of improving the costing system, it seems to me that the more units we sell of a particular product, the lower the per unit cost of that product should be. Once we have a product up and running, our support costs stay the same regardless of the number of units we sell."

Sid agrees: "The product costs vary with units sold, and order processing costs vary with number of orders, but most of the remaining indirect costs are fixed. Let's take a look at what we might do with those costs."

Sid then begins to suggest alternative ways of allocating indirect costs. Sean listens for a while before interrupting: "What you're suggesting is too complicated. I want something simple that everyone will understand. I want to get across the message that the more products we're carrying at any one time, the more it costs us, and that the more units we sell of one product, the less it costs us per unit." Sid says she will study the issue, and that brings the meeting to a close.

A few days later, Sid returns to Sean's office with new diagrams and charts. "Here's my suggested amendment to our costing system," she tells him. "First, I've allocated the indirect costs to each product. Our indirect costs are $150,000, and we have three products, so the 'support costs' of each product are $50,000. Then I've allocated the support costs to customers by dividing the $50,000 for each product by the number of units sold of each product. Using Product Alpha as an example, we would divide $50,000 by 500 units to get $100 per unit as a support cost. Here are the calculations for each of the products."

Indirect costs		$150,000	
Support costs per product		$50,000	

	Number of units	Per unit support costs
Alpha	500	$100
Beta	1,000	$50
Ceta	2,000	$25

She continues: "To find out what a customer costs us for a year we simply add together the direct product costs of the units they purchased, the support costs for the units they purchased, and the order costs for the number of orders they made. I've restated our 2004 results using the support cost amendment, and here's what we get."

Sean considers the figures in the "revised profits" row. "There's not as large a change in the profits as when we went to costing orders last year," he notes. "But that's not surprising. We're working with a smaller amount here. Still, there's some interesting results. Look at Veso. Your revised system tells us that Veso is half as profitable as we think it is. I wonder whether it's worth the hassle to change the system one more time."

Compware Financial Summary for 2004 with Support Allocations

	Veso	Western	Xero	Yavol	Zed	Totals
Revenue	83,704	184,630	244,815	199,815	237,037	950,000
Direct costs	45,000	90,000	135,000	110,000	120,000	500,000
Order costs	3,704	29,630	14,815	14,815	37,037	100,000
Product support costs	25,000	30,000	35,000	30,000	30,000	150,000
Total costs	73,704	149,630	184,815	154,815	187,037	750,000
"Revised" profits	**10,000**	**35,000**	**60,000**	**45,000**	**50,000**	**200,000**
"Reported" profits	21,784	35,848	56,345	43,450	42,573	200,000

Required

1. What signals does the amended system send?
2. Sean stated some objectives in amending the costing system. Will his objectives be achieved simply by providing new information, or should he consider fine tuning the performance measurement and reward system?
3. Should Compware adopt the new system?
4. How do you think Kris Apt, Compware's top salesperson, will react to another change in the costing system?

FUZZY DOGS

Tony Dimnik

Tofu is one of the main ingredients in Haute Dogs wieners. Haute Dog's production manager, Kris Ashar, approaches the company president, Cassandra McDonnell, with an idea to buy a new machine that would reduce the costs of seasoning the tofu mixture. The old seasoning machine has long ago been written off for both financial accounting and tax purposes and has zero market value.

Kris and Cassandra meet to discuss the purchase of the new machine, the Tofu-Master. Here is a transcript of their conversation:

Kris: Depending on negotiations with the manufacturer, we could get a Tofu-Master for anywhere between $30,000 and $35,000. I expect that a Tofu-Master will save us between $10,000 and $15,000 a year from more efficient use of seasonings and from reduced tofu wastage.

Cassandra: I think your estimates of savings are a bit optimistic. I figure $8,000 is a more realistic estimate.

Kris: OK. Let's assume that savings will probably be between $8,000 and $10,000 per year, although they might go as high as $15,000.

Cassandra: Fine. Looking at your proposal here, I notice that you think the Tofu-Master will be in service for ten years, after which it will have a salvage value of $10,000. I think five years and zero salvage value are more realistic estimates.

Kris: Yes, I guess you're probably right. We're sure we can use the Tofu-Master for five years. After that, who knows? But there is a growing market for used equipment, so I think it's realistic to assume that we'll be able to get about $10,000 for the Tofu-Master five years from now.

Cassandra: I still think that's too optimistic. But I do agree with your tax shield and tax rate estimates. We'll be able to claim a 20 percent CCA, and the tax rate will probably stay between 35 and 40 percent. However, I disagree with your working capital estimates. You've got inventories increasing by $8,000 and accounts payable increasing by $3,000. I think inventories might go up to $10,000, and it's unlikely our suppliers would carry us for more than $2,000.

Kris: Maybe, but I think that $5,000 is still the best estimate of the increase in working capital required by the Tofu-Master.

Cassandra: Good. One final point is the discount rate. We would usually use a 10 percent after-tax rate, but since this is a new technology for us, we should reflect the riskiness of the project by increasing the discount rate to say, 15 percent.

Kris: I'm not sure about that. We shouldn't be penalizing investments in new equipment. If anything we should be lowering the discount rate for promising new technologies. If we're ever going to move into other areas like tofu burgers, we'll have to experiment with the tofu mix. The Tofu-Master allows us to do that. Somehow we should factor in the possibility that by investing in the Tofu-Master, we will have a better opportunity to develop some new products.

Required

Prepare an analysis of the Tofu-Master investment decision.

MEDISIGHT CONSULTING CONTRACT BID

Tony Dimnik

Medisight is a successful Canadian-based medical imaging company. In February 2004 its senior management team met to discuss the merits and details of bidding on a contract to optimize and maintain twelve imaging machines, which the Ontario government had purchased in late 2003.

The Company

Medisight has four business units, each with its own general manager:

- *Research Unit* is headed by Richard Davies. It conducts basic and applied research on technologies that enable doctors to produce real-time detailed images of their patients' internal functions. It also monitors current and potential American and Canadian regulations for imaging technologies.
- *Operations Unit* is headed by Omar Ulbreth. It designs, manufactures, and sells imaging machines.
- *Consulting Unit* is headed by Corrine Bilodeau. It performs regular maintenance and optimization of machines, and also trains operators in basic and advanced procedures.
- *Administrative Support Unit* is headed by Adrian Sandow. It provides IT, HR, accounting, marketing, and other support services to the three other departments.

Medisight's basic model, the Insight-100, sells for $7,000,000 and as of 2003 has captured a significant share of the North American market.

By the late 1990s, medical institutions were beginning to outsource maintenance and training for their imaging technologies. By 2002, Medisight had set up its Consulting Unit to compete for that business. Medisight's management soon realized that the life cycle revenues generated by that unit had the potential to exceed the revenues from the Operations Unit.

The technology used by the Insight-100 had been developed by a team of doctors and scientists at Queen's University in the early 1990s. In 1997 the university established a company to exploit the technology. The company was privately owned by a diverse group of shareholders, including the university, members of the original Queen's team, the federal government, and the Ontario government's technology investment fund. The company has an independent board of directors.

Medisight's management has written a mission statement for the company. This statement notes that the company aims to be the top provider of hardware and services for medical imaging in Canada and one of the top three providers in North America. Medisight also has a vision statement, which references its commitment to patients, doctors, and shareholders as well as its intention to reinvest a significant portion of its profits in R&D.

The Industry

Medical imaging is a growing business in North America because of an aging population and governments' strengthening focus on cost-reducing technologies. Four organizations are competing against Medisight in various aspects of its business:

- *Ottawa University Technologies* (OUT). This is a consortium of scientists who are researching the next generation of imaging technologies. Their aim is to license their technologies to companies such as Medisight and its competitors.
- *General Medical Technologies* (GMT). This is an American multinational that offers both imaging hardware and consulting but licenses its technologies from organizations such as OUT and its American counterparts.
- *Medical Imaging Consultants* (MIC). This is a Canadian company that competes only on the consulting and maintenance side of the business.
- *European Diagnostics* (ED). This is a French multinational that operates in all three areas of the industry: research, manufacturing, and consulting.

Exhibit 1 shows the market shares of Medisight and its competitors in North America and the prospects for growth in the hardware and consulting businesses. Exhibit 2 is a size-up of each of the main players in the industry and has been prepared by Corrine Bilodeau, the general manager of the Consulting Unit.

Bidding on the Consulting Contract

In 2003, a one-time grant from the Canadian government allowed the Ontario government to purchase a total of twelve Insight-100s at a total cost of $80 million. The federal government is also prepared to subsidize the operating costs of the 12 machines. It has announced a March 15, 2004, deadline for bidding on a three-year consulting contract that is to include the training of operators and the optimization and maintenance of the machines.

On February 15, 2004, Peter Autenreid, the president of Medisight, meets in Toronto with the managers of the four divisions to discuss the bid on the consulting contract. Transcripts of portions of the meeting follow:

Peter: The first thing on the agenda is to decide whether or not we should even bid for this contract. It seems to me that we might be better off focusing on the richer American market than trying to compete for a piece of the smaller Canadian market.

Corrine: As you know, our consulting business is just starting to take off. If we can establish ourselves in our home market, we'll have a very good base to work from in attacking the American market. Our goal is to be number one in Canada, and we can't do that if we lose this contract. And one more point — our machines are expected to last for about ten years, so if we win this contract and do a good job, we will lock in our customers for another six or seven years after the contract is over. Our projections show that over the life of the machines, the consulting contracts will be worth $70 to $90 million.

Adrian: Let me show you two different versions of the projected income for the contract. The first version is Corrine's [see Exhibit 3]. As you can see, this contract only shows direct costs. Corrine hasn't included the 15 percent mark-ups for each business unit, which provide for the units' overheads and profits, and she hasn't included a 10 percent charge for the Administrative Support Unit. Also, as you know, our policy is to add 10 percent of costs as a contingency. I've revised Corrine's numbers, and as you can see [see Exhibit 4], the margins drop to 11 percent. Our bid price will have to be considerably higher to make the industry average margin of 20 percent.

Corrine: I appreciate what you're saying, but we can't go any higher or we'll lose the contract to MIC. I don't see why we have to have a 15 percent mark-up on business unit costs. There won't be any major increases in overhead costs. And there will only be a small increase in Adrian's costs — some extra accounting and some IT support, but that's it. I know that MIC will be really competitive on this bid. They'll be contracting out their research and parts, and I know that if they come to us we'll be selling to them at a lower price than you want to charge me. Our current business is already covering our overhead and our support costs, so as long as we cover our out-of-pocket costs, there shouldn't be a problem. Oh, and one final point, about the 10 percent contingency. I know we build that into our budgets for Research and Operations projects because those have a history of missing projections, but since salaries are our major cost and we have just signed a five-year contract with our union, our projections don't need a contingency.

Omar: It's fine to say that we are already covering our costs, but Adrian is right — your price should cover the full costs and a contingency. That's how we operate.

Corrine: If we price at full costs plus contingency plus a margin, we will never get the contract.

Peter: But if we don't do that, we can end up winning the contract and losing money.

Corrine: I have one other alternative. What if we were to price at full cost but offer deferred payment? Governments are always happy to postpone payments as long as possible. It will stretch our cash reserves, but I think it's doable. Here's what the contract would look like with deferred payments [see Exhibit 5].

Richard: Let me see if I understand these three projections correctly. Corrine's projections [Exhibit 3] are essentially cash flows. So the income in year 1 is really the cash flow that we expect from the consulting project in that year. In Adrian's projections [Exhibit 4], the mark-ups include a share of overhead expenses such as depreciation and a profit. And the third option [Exhibit 5] simply adjusts Adrian's projections to take into account the deferred payments.

Peter: That's how I understand it. We've got lots to think about. As you know, the board has asked us to go through a risk review process before we bid on a contract of this magnitude. If we want to make the March 15 deadline, we'll have to submit the proposal for an RRP by the end of February.

EXHIBIT 1: Market Information

Organization	Market Share of Hardware in North America (%)	Market Share of Consulting in North America (%)
Medisight	20	15
General Medical Technologies	45	40
Medical Imaging Consultants	0	20
European Diagnostics	35	25
	Projected Annual Growth Rates (2004–09) (%)	Estimated 2003 Margins on Sales (%)
Hardware	10	10
Consulting	15	20

Data in Exhibit 1 from International Review of Medical Imaging 2003.

EXHIBIT 2: Competitive Analysis

Medisight	• In-house R&D supported by business • Hardware and consulting service • Reputation for quality products but less well-known for consulting service • Competitive prices • Home base is in Canada and not in U.S. market • Access to well-trained Canadian engineers and doctors • Board tends to be conservative and risk averse • Not market leader in any segment
Ottawa University Technologies (OUT)	• Starting with clean slate — no legacy projects • Attracting some of the brightest new scientists • Does not sell "exclusives" and therefore has multiple revenue streams for each technology • Depends on fickle university and government funding • Little motivation to conduct commercially relevant research
General Medical Technologies (GMT)	• Buys research • Market leader in North America in both hardware and consulting • Bureaucratic and slow moving — reactive rather than proactive toward competition • Reputation for mediocre customer relations • Products and services considered overpriced

(Continued)

(*Continued*)

Medical Imaging Consultants (MIC)	• Excellent customer relations • Very aggressive in consulting business • Hires people from competitors (including Medisight) by offering commission-based compensation • Well funded • Has some trouble sourcing parts and keeping up to date on new technologies
European Diagnostics (ED)	• Focus is clearly on European business • Excellent technology but has to be adapted to North America • Hardware pricing is very aggressive • Lagging in consulting business because of difficulty in hiring qualified staff • Mediocre customer relations

EXHIBIT 3: Corrine's Consulting Contract Income Statement

	Year 1	Year 2	Year 3
Revenues	3,000,000	3,400,000	4,000,000
Consulting labour	1,000,000	1,200,000	1,500,000
Benefits	250,000	300,000	375,000
Mark-up	62,500	75,000	93,750
Operations materials	200,000	200,000	200,000
Mark-up	0	0	0
Operations labour	300,000	300,000	300,000
Benefits	75,000	75,000	75,000
Mark-up	18,750	18,750	18,750
R&D labour	100,000	100,000	100,000
Benefits	25,000	25,000	25,000
Mark-up	6,250	6,250	6,250
Administration charge	0	0	0
Plus contingency	0	0	0
Total costs	2,037,500	2,300,000	2,693,750
Income	962,500	1,100,000	1,306,250
Margin	32%	32%	33%

EXHIBIT 4: Adrian's Consulting Contract Income Statement

	Year 1	Year 2	Year 3
Revenues	3,000,000	3,400,000	4,000,000
Consulting labour	1,000,000	1,200,000	1,500,000
Benefits	250,000	300,000	375,000
Mark-up	187,500	225,000	281,250
Operations materials	200,000	200,000	200,000
Mark-up	30,000	30,000	30,000
Operations labour	300,000	300,000	300,000
Benefits	75,000	75,000	75,000
Mark-up	56,250	56,250	56,250
R&D labour	100,000	100,000	100,000
Benefits	25,000	25,000	25,000
Mark-up	18,750	18,750	18,750
Administration charge	300,000	340,000	400,000
Plus contingency	130,000	154,000	190,000
Total costs	2,672,500	3,024,000	3,551,250
Income	327,500	376,000	448,750
Margin	11%	11%	11%

EXHIBIT 5: Income Statement with Deferred Payments

	Year 1	Year 2	Year 3
Revenues	1,000,000	3,000,000	6,500,000
Consulting labour	1,000,000	1,200,000	1,500,000
Benefits	250,000	300,000	375,000
Mark-up	187,500	225,000	281,250
Operations materials	200,000	200,000	200,000
Mark-up	30,000	30,000	30,000
Operations labour	300,000	300,000	300,000
Benefits	75,000	75,000	75,000
Mark-up	56,250	56,250	56,250
R&D labour	100,000	100,000	100,000
Benefits	25,000	25,000	25,000
Mark-up	18,750	18,750	18,750
Administration charge	100,000	300,000	650,000
Plus contingency	110,000	150,000	215,000
Total costs	2,452,500	2,980,000	3,826,250
Income	(1,452,500)	20,000	2,673,750
Margin	(145%)	1%	41%

Required

1. Should Corrine's (Exhibit 3) or Adrian's (Exhibit 4) estimates serve as the basis of the consulting bid?
2. Use your best estimate of the income from the consulting contract to conduct a discounted cash flow analysis of the contract. There are three additional facts you should know:

   - If Medisight wins the bid, Operations will have to invest $1,000,000 in new equipment to support the contract.
   - Medisight uses a 10 percent hurdle rate for all its investments.
   - Medisight pays no income taxes.

3. Is the deferred payment plan a viable alternative?
4. What should Medisight do?

CHAPTER 6

A GUIDE TO ACTIVE/EXPERIENTIAL LEARNING

Tell me, I'll forget.
Show me, I may remember.
But involve me, and I'll understand.[1]

As we discussed in Chapter 1, management accounting and management account-ants are intimately involved in strategic decision making in organizations. Unlike financial statements, which may become public documents for use by anonymous stakeholders, management accounting information is used primarily within the organization. In this context, face-to-face interaction is common and management accounting information becomes the basis for coordinating and negotiating actions. Furthermore, management accounting information is future- and goal-oriented and is produced through the active involvement of many people in the organization. For example, it is impossible to produce a budget without gathering information from every unit in the organization regarding estimated costs and activity levels. Part of your education in management accounting, therefore, must include gaining an understanding of how management accounting information is developed and used through interactions with others.

In Chapter 7 we will present a series of active learning exercises that will provide you with insights into how organizations assemble and use management accounting information. Active learning is an approach that combines four stages or types of learning into one rich experience.[2] Honey and Mumford (1982)[3] have suggested that there are four styles of students in terms of how they prefer to perceive the world and how they process information about that world. Regarding perception, some students prefer concrete experience (e.g., examples) whereas others are more comfortable with theory and conceptual explanations. In terms of processing information, some students prefer to reflect on information and try to make it "fit" with other things they

---

[1] The source of this proverb is obscure. It has been attributed to both Chinese and Native American oral history.

[2] D.A. Kolb, *Experiential Learning* (Englewood Cliffs, NJ: Prentice-Hall, 1984).

[3] P. Honey and A. Mumford, *Manual of Learning Styles* (London: P. Honey, 1982).

FIGURE 6.1: Learning Styles (after Honey and Mumford, 1982; Kolb, 1984)

		Preferred Way of Getting New Information	
		Concrete Experience (feeling)	Abstract Concepts (thinking)
Preferred way of testing your understanding	Reflection (watching)	Reflectors	Theorists
	Action (doing)	Activists	Pragmatists

know, whereas others prefer to jump in immediately and try things out. These two dimensions can be combined to identify four different learning styles. See if you recognize yourself in Figure 6.1.

- *Reflectors*. Prefer direct experience with new knowledge. That is, they prefer examples, visual aides, and case studies, and then like to sit back and think about what they have learned.
- *Theorists*. Prefer high-level general introductions to new knowledge. They are comfortable being told theories and concepts without being required to anchor these in day-to-day examples. Then they think about the new concepts and use their imagination to see how they fit into other things they know.
- *Activists*. Prefer direct experience with new knowledge. They prefer examples, visual aides, and case studies, and then like to immediately try out their new knowledge.
- *Pragmatists*. Prefer high-level general introductions to new knowledge. They are comfortable being told theories and concepts without being required to anchor them in day-to-day examples. Then they think about these concepts and use their imagination to see how they fit into other things they know.

Each of these learning styles is valid, and in your class there will be people who are in each of these categories. The challenge for instructors is how to help each type of student learn about management accounting!

Kolb (1984) has suggested that active learning can do just that by combining four types of learning into one experience. Active learning has four stages, which together form a cycle that can be entered at any point. This means that your instructor may choose to use the materials in this book with lectures in a variety of equally valid ways (e.g., a simulation may be used before or after concepts are introduced in a lecture). The four stages are:

1. having concrete experience of a phenomenon;
2. observing and reflecting on experience;
3. forming abstract generalizations (creating theory); then
4. testing generalizations in new situations.

These four stages provide opportunities for concrete experience, reflection, theorization, and action. In an action learning environment, you will experience

FIGURE 6.2: Learning Styles and Active Learning

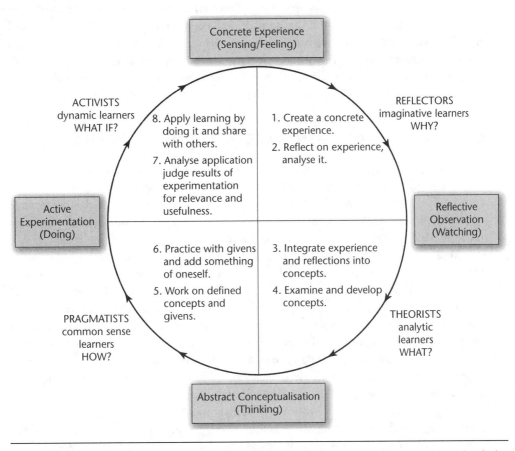

Source: David Kolb, *Experiential Learning: Experience as a Source of Learning,* © 1984, p. 42. Adapted with the permission of Pearson Education, Inc., Upper Saddle River, NJ.

management accounting in many ways, at *least* one of which should help you achieve the level of understanding you need to succeed. Figure 6.2 summarizes the learning styles and the stages of experiential learning.

Beyond our concern for helping people of every learning style succeed in this course, we have two reasons for this approach. First, as the proverb we used to introduce this chapter suggests, being involved in the process will help you gain a level of understanding of management accounting that you cannot achieve through lectures and demonstration problems. Instead of being a passive recipient of information, you will actively apply the information in a context that captures the essence of how information is used in organizations. When you engage with management accounting information in this way, it is not enough to memorize procedures or formulas; you must integrate this knowledge with its application to decision problems and use the information creatively in order to achieve your goals.

Second, by creating situations in which you can interact with others, we are also providing an opportunity for you to understand the variability in human behaviour. In negotiations, for example, people may behave competitively or cooperatively; they may behave rationally or emotionally; they may be persuaded by logic, by an appeal to role models and precedents, or by claims to fairness or other values. Each time you engage in negotiations, even when the circumstances appear the same, the process and outcomes may differ. You need to allow for these variations in interactions instead of assuming that people will always be the same.

SUCCESS IN MANAGEMENT ACCOUNTING EXERCISES

When you participate in these exercises, the key to "success" (i.e., to learning as much as you can from the experience) will be to take on the role that is assigned to you. In case analysis, the "required" section of the case provides you with the perspective from which your analysis is to be conducted and reported. In simulations you must take this role play to a new level and be ready to interact while "in the role."

Role plays are being used more and more often in business. They are used in interviews to determine whether potential employees possess the skills required for a position. For example, when hiring customer service personnel, the interviewer can take on the role of a disgruntled customer and see how the candidate would handle pressure. Role plays are also used to train employees and managers to handle anticipated situations. For example, a senior manager presenting evidence to a regulatory commission or in a court case will be prepared by a lawyer, who may role play the cross-examination to ensure that the manager can handle typical and unusual questions while staying "on message."

To get the most out of a role play, you should follow some simple guidelines. First, understand the role you are playing. Think through the responsibilities of the position you are taking on as well as the incentives/pressures, both monetary and social, affecting that position. Second, understand the situation in which you are interacting and how it might affect a person in this role. Feel free to be creative, but stay in character.

The active learning exercises in this book are of two types. First, we provide a number of exercises that encourage you or a small group to work together to develop a proposal or other information. You will then be able to compare the approach you have used with others in the class to better understand where choices have been made and how people vary in their approach to situations. Second, we provide exercises where you will interact directly with others in the class as part of the simulation. Typically these are situations where each person will have information that is specific to him or her and will be negotiating with a second party that has its own unique set of information.

Simulations that create a context in which you use management accounting information to negotiate on behalf of yourself (e.g., for a pay raise) or on behalf of your organization (e.g., when arranging a supply contract) provide you with the closest experience of the real use of management accounting information that we can provide. All of us have experienced negotiations in our personal lives; however, you may not have been exposed to any guidance on how to conduct a negotiation. So that your use of these simulations will be as rewarding as possible, we provide this brief overview of negotiation theory to help you.

THE ESSENCE OF NEGOTIATION

Negotiation is one of the core functions of management. There are many models of the negotiation process. Some of these models rely on game theory and try to develop strategies based on the structure of a problem; other models try to capture the process through which negotiations typically unfold in order to identify the skills needed. This is not the place to provide a complete review of the extensive literature on negotiations. For our purposes it is enough to provide a basic overview.

Negotiations take place in different circumstances, and it is important to understand which circumstance you are in before trying to negotiate an outcome. For example, sometimes negotiations are undertaken simply to coordinate action. Here there is no right or wrong, no winner or loser, but we must agree on what we are doing. For example, in some countries cars drive on the right side of the road while other countries use the left side of the road. As drivers we need to coordinate our actions and agree which side of the road we are going to drive on. This will require some initial negotiation, but we should be able to agree. Someone from North America who arrives in England and rents a car may be tempted to renegotiate this agreement with other drivers on the road; very quickly, though, he or she will find that changing driving habits is the most sensible response to the circumstances.

At other times, negotiations are undertaken in a "distributive"[4] bargaining context — that is, the negotiation is about how a fixed resource is to be distributed among the negotiating parties. Game theorists refer to these situations as zero-sum (win/lose) games. For example, when you are negotiating the price of some item at the market, every penny less you pay (a win for you) is also a penny less the vendor earns (a loss for them). The negotiation then has to do with the alternatives each party has (e.g., can you buy somewhere else; other people will want to buy the good) and with the preferences each person has (e.g., there are other ways you could spend the money). The success of your negotiating skills in these situations can be defined simply in terms of your gains versus someone else's losses.

Finally, negotiation may be undertaken in an "integrative" bargaining context where, through collaboration, the parties attempt to negotiate a change in their behaviours or interactions that will benefit both. Game theorists refer to these as non–zero-sum (win/win) games. In many manufacturing situations, for example, it

---

[4] The distinction between distributive bargaining and integrative bargaining is made by R.E. Walton and R.B. McKersie, *A Behavioral Theory of Labor Negotiation* (New York: McGraw-Hill, 1965).

has been found that involving suppliers in the design of products can result in lower costs for components and higher profits for both the supplier and the manufacturer.[5] The negotiation is about finding a solution that will maximize the joint payoff for both parties. Of course, it is possible that some alternatives will be better for one party than the other even though both gain!

One difficulty in negotiations is that it may not be clear which situation prevails. Sometimes, the mental model that participants bring to the table can become a self-fulfilling prophecy. Consider the example above of a supplier negotiating with a manufacturer. If both parties see the problem as a distributive bargaining issue, then the key to success becomes developing alternatives (the supplier will seek new customers and differentiate their products in search of higher margins; the customer will seek multiple suppliers and encourage competition among them in order to force price reductions) and information will be carefully guarded to avoid giving the other party insights into the "bottom line" negotiating position. It will be difficult in this situation to change behaviours to support integrative bargaining. If, however, both parties see the problem as an integrative bargaining situation, the behaviour will be totally different. Information will be shared, and each party will seek to develop a relationship so that trust can develop. In an integrative bargaining context, the key is to find ways to make the pie bigger rather than fighting about who gets the biggest slice of the pie.

Many of the simulations that follow require you to enter into a negotiation or bargaining situation. You will have to decide which type of negotiation situation it is and how you should orient yourself within it; your bargaining partners will be making the same decisions and their assessments may not be the same as yours depending on the unique information they hold. In many situations, bargaining will be more effective if you start from principles rather than positions.[6] Your position is what you want. Your bargaining partner will also have a position. When stated in these terms, the negotiation is immediately about conflict between these two positions. An alternative is to think in terms of principles — that is, the values you bring to the table — rather than the place where you want to end up. For example, you and a vendor may both agree that you would like to exchange an item at a price that is fair to both parties; there is now a mutual problem to be solved, instead of conflicting positions about how much one person is willing to pay versus how much another person is willing to accept.

Negotiating is a complex process (your school probably has entire courses devoted to the theory and practice of negotiations). The instructions below should be seen as a simplified way to approach the tasks we will be setting for you in this book. As your negotiating skills and knowledge improve throughout your career, you can revisit these exercises and consider what you might have done differently. When reading the simulation instructions, here is what you should do to prepare yourself.

---

[5] This is an important aspect of "target costing" processes, in which products are redesigned to meet cost constraints in cooperation with the entire supply chain.

[6] R. Fisher and W. Ury, *Getting to Yes: Negotiating Agreement Without Giving In* (New York: Penguin, 1983).

1. Define your goals.
   a. The instructions will specify which role you are playing and provide you with the background to the negotiation you are entering.
   b. Identify why you are entering the negotiation, and specify for yourself what you would consider an acceptable outcome.
2. Be prepared.
   a. Negotiations are about using information.
   b. Carefully consider all the information available, and where possible use the information to analyze your situation and the situation facing your bargaining partner.
   c. Understand what the best alternative is to a negotiated agreement (BATNA); this will help you understand what's at stake!
   d. Set your limits; know the range of acceptable alternatives.
   e. Understand the role that informal norms (e.g., fairness) and ethics (e.g., will you lie to secure the best deal for yourself?) play in your interaction.
3. Consider your strategy.
   a. Try to understand the situation and anticipate how your negotiating partner will understand the situation.
   b. If it is a distributive bargaining situation, here are some possible strategies:
      i. Make an extreme offer and then back away to where you are comfortable.
      ii. Downplay the importance of the issue to you (e.g., by developing alternatives).
      iii. Alternate hard bargaining with friendly concessions.
      iv. Bluff – use threats to make the other party make concessions, or misrepresent your interests.
      v. Give ultimatums – but be prepared to lose.
   c. If it is an integrative bargaining situation, here are some possible strategies.
      i. Look for opportunities to expand the payoffs (i.e., to make the pie bigger for everyone).
      ii. Share information.
      iii. Build trust in the relationship. (This provides a context for creativity and information sharing. Trust allows you to take personal risks, such as suggesting things that make you vulnerable or giving information away about your weaknesses, without fear that your bargaining partner will take advantage.)
      iv. Look for mutually satisfying agreements (i.e., find out what your partner wants and make sure that the alternatives meet these needs).
4. Close the deal.
   a. Get an agreement that can be monitored and enforced (if necessary).
   b. Ensure that post-agreement dissonance is managed (i.e., each party must continue to be happy with the bargain reached).
5. Have fun! Remember that these are learning exercises. Please take the learning objectives seriously without becoming too serious about the roles you are playing or the ways that others may have interpreted their roles.

CHAPTER 7

ACTIVE LEARNING EXERCISES

The exercises in this chapter are divided into two sections. The first section includes five exercises that require you to complete the exercise as part of a group and then share your results with others. These exercises contain all the information you will need to complete the exercise. The exercises in this section are:

- Getting a Summer Job: Activity-Based Management
- Student Recruiting: A Capital Budgeting Approach
- Markle College: Request for Proposal
- The MBA Grad Formal: Target Costing
- Lea Pets: Customer Profitability Analysis

The second section includes eight exercises that require you to interact with others and negotiate an agreement. In some of these exercises, each person will be given additional and unique information in order to establish his or her role in the exercise. Do not share this information with others until you understand your role and decide whether or not sharing information will help you achieve your goal in the exercise. You should read Chapter 6 before beginning these exercises; doing so will provide you with some background on negotiations. The exercises in this section are:

- Kumar Integration/Mazierski Software: Project Bidding
- Horvath Chemicals: Activity-Based Budgeting (A) and (B)
- York Wireless
- Farrell Lighting: Activity-Based Budgeting
- Car Buyer's Dilemma
- Technoration
- Reorganizing Hospital Services

GETTING A SUMMER JOB: ACTIVITY-BASED MANAGEMENT

Charles Plant

You have been hired by a youth summer employment program to conduct a major project to implement "activity-based management."[1] As part of that project, you are attempting to identify what students must do to get a summer job and how to recognize when their job search is going well.

To complete this study, you are required to interview two students. Gather the following information about their last attempt to get a summer job:

1. Determine what activities the student undertook to find a job, and break these activities into specific tasks (e.g., an activity may be "prepare a résumé," which includes the tasks of identifying an appropriate format, gathering information, drafting the resume, proofreading, etc.).
2. Identify the resources needed for each task.
3. For each activity, define an output measure (i.e., what was produced).
4. For each activity, define a performance measure (i.e., how would you determine the quality of the outputs?).
5. Record the actual performance achieved by the student.
6. Brainstorm improvement ideas:

   • Identify any tasks that were unnecessary and could be eliminated.
   • Identify tasks that were necessary but could be done better (i.e., more efficiently or with better results).
   • Identify tasks that were not done but would have improved the job search.

Required

1. When you have completed these steps and have filled in the sheet on the following page, try to determine ways in which the job search process could be improved.
2. As a group, compare your activity models and make suggestions for improvement.

---

[1] Activity-based management (ABM) refers to the use of information about processes, tasks, and activities to identify the efficiency and effectiveness of workplace operations. It is common in ABM to distinguish between value-adding and non-value-adding activities. Those activities which do not add value (and are not of strategic importance or legally required) can be eliminated to release resources for other uses or to reduce costs.

Activity	Task	Resources	Output Measure	Performance Measure	Actual Performance

STUDENT RECRUITING: A CAPITAL BUDGETING APPROACH

Charles Plant

You are in charge of recruiting MBA students for your school. You have been approached by a student who wants you to use capital budgeting techniques to help her determine where she should take her MBA.

This student currently lives in Toronto, where she has completed her BBA at Ryerson with very high marks and high GMATs. The student has been working for two years at a small chartered accounting firm and will finish her CA designation shortly. She currently earns $52,000 per year. The student is considering five different MBA programs: Wharton in Pennsylvania, Stanford in California, Insead in Switzerland, Rotman in Toronto, and Schulich in Toronto.[2] She has collected the following data from a current MBA ranking survey in the *Financial Times*.[3]

Overall Rank	Program	Salary after 3 Years	Tuition $CDN	Career Progress Rank	Placement Success Rank	International Mobility Rank
1	Wharton	$171,000	$96,000	48	20	61
4	Stanford	180,000	86,000	26	22	57
8	Insead	145,000	81,000	9	69	7
21	Rotman	113,000	53,000	50	55	54
22	Schulich	102,000	35,000	7	78	30
	Other?					

The following information pertains to the various categories in the chart.

1. The overall rank is the final ranking on the MBA ranking, which covers 100 universities.
2. The salary after three years is the total of salary and bonuses earned by the average graduate in the third year after graduation. The student currently earns $52,000, and you can assume that first-year salary will be 70 percent of third-year salary and that the second year will be 85 percent of third year. Ignore the time value of money in calculations; we will focus on "payback" as the criterion — that is, the number of years of work it takes to pay back the cost of the program. (You may extend the analysis by using other criteria.)
3. Tuition is the total cost of a two-year program. If the student studies outside of Toronto, it will cost an extra $40,000 for two years' living expenses.
4. Career Progress Rank is the degree to which alumni have moved up the career ladder three years after graduating. Progression is measured through changes in level of seniority and in the size of the employing company.

---

[2] You should add to this table the data for your school, if available, or choose one of the listed schools as the focus of your analysis.

[3] From the Financial Times 2005 Global MBA Ranking, http://specials.ft.com/spdocs/be2005_globalmba_2005.pdf.

5. Placement Success Rank is the percentage of alumni who gained employment with the help of career advice. The data are presented as a rank.
6. International Mobility Rank is a rating system that measures the degree of international mobility. It is based on the employment movements of alumni between graduation and today.

Required

Use the criteria listed above, or any other criteria you can think of, to convince the student to go to your school. Prepare a chart formatted with the headings shown below, and be prepared to defend your criteria in a presentation to the entire class.

Choosing Your School as Capital Budgeting Problem

Anticipated results
Payback analysis
Risk factors
Non-financial factors
Recommendation
Justification

MARKLE COLLEGE: REQUEST FOR PROPOSAL

Charles Plant

Markle College, a new community college specializing in teaching financial accounting, has just issued a request for proposal (RFP) for the provision of computers and software for a new teaching lab. The request covers four items:

- *Computers.* The lab requires one supervisory and 60 networked desktop computers. The configuration of these computers is similar to the average computer supplied by your firm. Of the four elements of the bid, this element is of the least importance to the college.
- *Software.* The purpose of the lab is to teach financial accounting, and the contract calls for the provision of custom software development. The new software to be created will provide interactive instruction to help students make accounting entries. It has been estimated that this software development will take 785 hours. As the college's reputation is based on its teaching ability, this part of the bid is the most important.
- *Installation and training.* As part of the project, you will be required to install and test all computers and train all of Markle's staff to use the software. This component of the project should take your installation and training staff 1,675 hours. Installation can be done in three different waves under three different projects and could last a whole year. Or it could all be done in one four-month project. The client would prefer that the work be done in one project but understands the difficulties this might entail. The quality of installation and training is important, but this ranks below software and support in importance.
- *Support.* You will be required to support this installation and the software over the next year. You have estimated that this activity will take 305 hours. This component of the bid is the second most important component, as the college wants speedy resolution of problems so that the students will not be affected by computer or software down time.

Markle College is expecting bids less than $400,000. This is a competitive bidding process, and you are especially eager to win the bid. Your objective as a firm is to earn a contribution margin from operations of 40 percent. Markle College has a full disclosure policy, which means that you will be required as part of the bid to show all of your costs.

In preparing the bid, you have accumulated the following background data. The attached financial statements show the results of your company's operations for the previous year.

- *Computer revenue.* Revenue was from the sale of 372 computers from 19 clients. All of the computers you sold last year were outsourced from another supplier.
- *Software.* This revenue was from all 19 clients and was all created internally by your software team. The team consists of one manager and six programmers. The manager earns about $115,000 with bonuses. In total, the six programmers billed 8,973 hours

out of a total reasonable potential of 9,000 hours. (While they work 2,000 hours per year each, it is not reasonable to assume that they will bill more than 1,500 hours each.)

- *Installation and training.* Last year your firm undertook 27 projects for the 19 clients. In some cases you have several orders in a year from a client, causing the number of projects to be greater than the number of clients. Your team consists of one manager and nine staff, who do installation and training. The manager earns $92,000 with bonuses. In total, the nine staff billed 11,765 hours last year out of a total potential of 13,500.
- *Support.* Support revenue was earned from 67 clients who have purchased systems from you in the past several years. In total, they have 1,275 PCs deployed. The support team consists of one manager and six staff. While billing was fixed, they used 6,977 out of 9,000 potential billable hours in conducting the support. The manager earned about $90,000 last year.

In analyzing your firm's data, you have determined that regarding this bid, it is possible to change slightly the way the firm conducts its business. It will then be able to improve its quality or reduce the cost. The following are different ways to affect quality, cost, and timing.

- *Computers.* Your firm has been approached by a new computer supplier that specializes in orders with a quantity greater than 50. This supplier is prepared to set a price of $1,750 for orders of more than 50 units delivered once in the year. While the quality is acceptable, using a different product would increase time for installation, training, and support on the contract by 5 percent.
- *Software.* Regarding the completion of the software, your current staff is maxed out on projects. As a result, you have a number of choices.

    1. You could subcontract the software completion to a contractor, who would take about 850 hours to complete the work at a price of $60 per hour. This option would increase support costs by about 5 percent.
    2. Alternatively, you could hire a new programmer to do the work. As business is growing, the firm could probably absorb the new programmer.
    3. Finally, you could hire a new programmer to work on regular work and give this job to your top programmer. She could do the work in 650 hours, or she could spend the extra time to add all sorts of desirable features to the product.

- *Installation and training.* If the installation and training are done as three projects over the course of a year, you could hire a person for the year at a cost of $45,000 just to do this work. If the work is done in one project, you would likely have to hire another individual for the firm and have a number of people do the installation and training.
- *Support.* Your support team is fairly underutilized, so the addition of one person to the team to do this work would not be necessary, even with normal growth. However, you could improve service levels by adding a new dedicated person at a cost of $55,000 per year.

Required

Prepare a response to this RFP. In your response you will be required to:

(a) propose a fixed price for each item requested, along with a total price for the contract; *and*

(b) show all costs and revenues used to arrive at the pricing you propose as well as the profit you expect to earn.

MARKLE COLLEGE – FINANCIAL STATEMENTS

	Jan 04	Feb 04	Mar 04	Apr 04	May 04	Jun 04	Jul 04	Aug 04	Sep 04	Oct 04	Nov 04	Dec 04	TOTAL
Revenue Sources													
Computers	45,320	143,675	79,070	119,114	55,542	125,267	48,101	69,755	56,919	110,810	50,005	213,319	1,116,897
Software	154,447	99,894	72,908	33,075	173,155	128,994	32,994	72,233	112,278	30,375	58,500	107,361	1,076,214
Installation and Training	87,230	89,387	83,008	87,818	62,602	93,962	92,806	72,554	55,325	66,520	74,681	71,067	936,960
Support	59,587	88,667	120,249	41,469	54,347	149,975	76,857	50,297	71,957	97,359	102,152	166,208	1,079,124
Total Revenue	346,584	421,623	355,235	281,476	345,646	498,198	250,758	264,839	296,479	305,064	285,338	557,955	4,209,195
Cost of Computers Sold	(36,256)	(112,067)	(64,047)	(89,336)	(45,544)	(103,972)	(38,961)	(55,804)	(44,966)	(91,972)	(42,004)	(177,055)	(901,984)
Gross Margin	310,328	309,556	291,188	192,140	300,102	394,226	211,797	209,035	251,513	213,092	243,334	380,900	3,307,211
Software Development													
Salaries	52,899	52,899	52,899	52,899	52,899	52,899	52,899	52,899	52,899	52,899	52,899	52,899	634,788
Program Expense	3,245	1,297	3,108	2,675	2,715	3,087	2,186	1,687	1,395	1,459	1,727	3,046	27,627
	(56,144)	(54,196)	(56,007)	(55,574)	(55,614)	(55,986)	(55,085)	(54,586)	(54,294)	(54,358)	(54,626)	(55,945)	(662,415)
Installation and Training													
Salaries	42,146	41,235	43,987	41,658	40,589	40,986	42,389	41,253	41,982	43,987	39,453	40,281	499,946
Program Expense	1,057	2,967	4,532	1,073	983	1,125	1,592	1,143	1,359	1,862	1,092	2,563	21,348
	(43,203)	(44,202)	(48,519)	(42,731)	(41,572)	(42,111)	(43,981)	(42,396)	(43,341)	(45,849)	(40,545)	(42,844)	(521,294)
Support													
Salaries	39,193	40,452	38,176	41,678	39,857	41,739	39,822	40,583	39,166	39,498	40,765	41,766	482,695
Program Expense	1,784	1,653	1,046	2,309	1,232	1,076	1,743	1,632	1,591	1,333	1,097	2,452	18,948
	(40,977)	(42,105)	(39,222)	(43,987)	(41,089)	(42,815)	(41,565)	(41,215)	(40,757)	(40,831)	(41,862)	(44,218)	(501,643)

(Continued)

MARKLE COLLEGE–FINANCIAL STATEMENTS (Continued)

	Jan 04	Feb 04	Mar 04	Apr 04	May 04	Jun 04	Jul 04	Aug 04	Sep 04	Oct 04	Nov 04	Dec 04	TOTAL
Sales & Marketing													
S & M Salaries	55,574	55,574	55,574	55,574	55,574	55,574	55,574	55,574	55,574	55,574	55,574	55,574	666,888
Marketing & Communications	6,263	13,996	40,094	9,996	23,547	4,696	12,367	12,593	4,724	6,711	8,377	12,087	155,451
Commissions	8,157	3,358	9,966	1,209	4,963	3,211	2,325	3,750	3,058	1,739	4,508	4,427	50,671
Corporate Travel	0	0	8,973	1,708	5,498	9,091	−15	6,138	1,399	2,398	6,868	13,833	55,891
	(69,994)	(72,928)	(114,607)	(68,487)	(89,582)	(72,572)	(70,251)	(78,055)	(64,755)	(66,422)	(75,327)	(85,921)	(928,901)
General and Admin													
G & A Salaries	18,590	18,141	18,497	17,820	17,947	17,518	18,376	17,657	19,044	18,374	18,012	19,937	219,913
Telephone	906	1,399	1,847	1,371	1,576	1,905	1,491	1,862	1,350	1,300	1,449	1,520	17,976
Internet	2,216	3,930	1,970	1,976	1,991	1,965	2,006	1,965	1,965	1,965	1,965	1,965	25,879
Accounting and Legal	475	0	100	0	0	1,699	200	0	911	0	100	28,900	32,385
Professional Development	154	360	0	119	3,913	190	0	0	357	408	360	7,898	13,759
Rent	4,855	4,855	4,855	4,855	4,855	4,855	4,855	4,855	4,855	4,855	4,855	4,855	58,260
Other	663	1,002	1,104	1,428	2,534	1,136	947	1,323	1,338	2,192	1,654	1,138	16,459
	(27,859)	(29,687)	(28,373)	(27,569)	(32,816)	(29,268)	(27,875)	(27,662)	(29,820)	(29,094)	(28,395)	(66,213)	(384,631)
Profit before Tax	**72,151**	**66,438**	**4,460**	**−46,208**	**39,429**	**151,474**	**−26,960**	**−35,879**	**18,546**	**−23,462**	**2,579**	**85,760**	**308,327**

THE MBA GRAD FORMAL: TARGET COSTING

Charles Plant

This simulation has two parts. In the first part, the class will be broken into groups. Your job is to design a perfect grad formal using only certain information. Read your specific instructions and act accordingly.

In the second part, you will be given more information. Then, working as a group, you will be required to develop a plan using target costing. **Do not proceed to the second part until directed to do so by your instructor.**

The MBA Grad Formal: Target Costing (A)

You have just been assigned the job of designing the perfect MBA Grad evening. The potential costs for the different features shown here are per couple. Use the following feature options to design what you feel would be an excellent grad evening.

Item	Low Price Feature	Price	Mid Price Feature	Price	High Price Feature	Price
Transportation	Subway	$10	Taxi	$50	Limo	$100
Flowers	Daisies	10	Roses	20	Corsage	40
Dinner	Lasagna	40	Chicken	50	Steak	60
Speeches	The Dean	0	"Pinball"		"J Lo"	10
			Clements	5		
On screen	Slides	0	+ Music	5	Video	10
Drinks	Beer	40	Wine	50	Martinis	60
Dancing	DJ	10	Videos	20	Band	40
Total		$110		$200		$320

Required

Fill out the following chart to show your design for the perfect evening.

Item	Feature	Price per couple
Transportation		
Flowers		
Dinner		
Speeches		
On screen		
Drinks		
Dancing		
Total		

What criteria did you use in the design process? How did you handle trade-offs between cost and the features selected?

The MBA Grad Formal: Target Costing (B)

Do not attempt this exercise until you have completed "The MBA Grad Formal: Target Costing (A)." The experience you gained in the first case will help you appreciate the benefits of target costing.

You have just received a proposal from the MBA formal committee regarding the grad formal. They have proposed an evening consisting of the following features:

Item	Feature	Price per couple	Component cost
Transportation	Limo	$100	43%
Flowers	Roses	20	8
Dinner	Steak	60	26
Speeches	Pamela Anderson	5	2
On screen	Boring pictures	0	0
Drinks	Beer	40	17
Dancing	Video DJ	10	4
Total		$235	100%

Your job, should you decide to accept it, is to design the perfect MBA grad formal evening using target costing. Remember, there's no accounting for taste so we do not recommend or endorse any set of activities shown in this exercise.

A recent survey showed that the price your cash-starved fellow students would be willing to pay for a romantic grad formal for two, including all costs for transportation, the event, and generous amounts of alcohol, would be between $200 and $225 per couple for the whole evening. Further research has shown the following ranking of components; the raw scores rank the importance of each component of the perfect evening from Not Important (1) to Very Important (5), with 2, 3, and 4 being in between.

Customer requirement	Raw score	Ranking (%)
A sense of style	3	21
Being entertained	4	29
Unwinding	2	14
Whatever	5	36
Total	14	100

The following chart shows how each component of the formal contributes to the needs of the target market. In the Style component, for example, 50 percent comes from the method of transportation and 50 percent from the flowers. To determine how style relates to the component ranking, multiply the Styles ranking percentage of 21 percent by the effect on Transportation of 50 percent. Add to that the same calculations that relate to Transportation for Unwinding and Whatever. Compute a component ranking from this chart.

	Style (21%)	Entertain (29%)	Unwinding (14%)	Whatever (36%)	Component ranking
Transportation	50	–	10	10	**15.5**
Flowers	50	–	–	10	
Dinner	–	40	20	–	
Speeches	–	15	–	–	
Slide show	–	15	10	–	
Drinks	–	–	50	40	
Dancing	–	30	10	40	
Total	100	100	100	100	100

Figure out the action you need to take. The component ranking is from the previous chart. The value index is computed as column 3 divided by column 2. Where the value index is above "1," you will need to enhance the element; where it is below "1," you will need to reduce the cost.

	Component cost	Component ranking	Value index	Action
Transportation	43%	15.5%	**.36**	**Reduce**
Flowers	8			
Dinner	26			
Speeches	2			
Slide show	0			
Drinks	17			
Dancing	4			
Total	100%			

Calculate target cost by multiplying the total expected cost of $225 by the component ranking. Figure out your cost gaps.

	Component ranking	Target cost	Current cost	Gap
Transportation	43	**$ 34.88**	$100	**$65.12**
Flowers	8		20	
Dinner	26		60	
Speeches	2		5	
Slide show	0		0	
Drinks	17		40	
Dancing	4		10	
Total	100		$235	

Following are the choices for the evening in terms of optional features.

Item	Low Price		Mid Price		High Price	
	Feature	Price	Feature	Price	Feature	Price
Transportation	Subway	$10	Taxi	$50	Limo	$100
Flowers	Daisies	10	Roses	20	Corsage	40
Dinner	Lasagna	40	Chicken	50	Steak	60
Speeches	Dean	0	Pinball	5	J Lo	10
On screen	Slides	0	+ Music	5	Video	10
Drinks	Beer	40	Wine	50	Martinis	60
Dancing	DJ	10	Videos	20	Band	40
Total		$ 110		$ 200		$ 320

Required

Design the perfect grad evening according to the information provided above. Then compare this result to the result from Part A of this case. Explain the differences.

Item	Feature	Price per couple
Transportation		
Flowers		
Dinner		
Speeches		
On screen		
Drinks		
Dancing		
Total		

LEA PETS: CUSTOMER PROFITABILITY ANALYSIS

Charles Plant

Along with many other products, your company manufactures and sells Lea Pets to four target retail markets. These products are similar to Chia Pets. The target markets are Gardeners, Hobbyists, Jokers, and Art Collectors. Your company is one of many (over 10) in a highly disorganized and competitive market. You currently sell 5,000 units per year but have the capacity to manufacture and sell up to 8,000. Selling Lea pets into a market is important for the success of your other products, as the popularity of this product can influence sales of other products.

Currently, you are selling to all four markets, but the marketing cost of $2,000 per year per market is destroying your profitability. To improve your company performance, you will have to focus on only one of the four target market segments. Currently there is demand for only 50,000 Lea Pets, 12,500 in each of the four markets. You know that all of your competitors are planning a similar strategy of market dominance and that each competitor will be picking only one target market to go after. You will also need to establish a price to charge to potential customers in the market you choose. The lowest price in a market will sell 8,000 units, and the next lowest price will sell 4,500 units. Anyone else in the market will make no sales of this product. Here are the details about the four markets.

Target market	Price	COGS	# of orders per year	# of items returned per year	Warranty claims per year
Gardeners	5	3.5	5	400	500
Hobbyists	6	4.2	10	300	600
Jokers	4	2.8	20	500	200
Art Collectors	7	4.9	40	900	300
Cost Per			$40.00	$1.00	$2.00

Required

The class will be divided into teams for this exercise.

1. Use the cost data provided to evaluate the profitability of each of the target markets.
2. Choose the target market you want to go after.
3. Figure out what price you want to charge for your Lea Pets in your target market.
4. Summarize your decision according to the following headings:

   Company (Create a name for your company)

   Target Market (Identify the one market that you would target)

   Price (Decide on the price that you would charge)

5. Your instructor will collect and summarize your decisions. Note: Your success will depend on both your decisions *and* the decisions of other teams.

KUMAR INTEGRATION/MAZIERSKI SOFTWARE: PROJECT BIDDING

Charles Plant

Kumar Integration, a small local systems integrator, has just lost a bid for a contract to develop a Customer Relationship Management software subsystem for a new client. The client, Morales Toys, has notified Kumar that the bid has been won by a large firm, Mazierski Software, which already does a lot of work for Morales.

Soon after this, Mazierski's project manager determines that his firm does not have all the resources it needs to complete the project. While it could complete the project itself, it wants to consider the option of subcontracting.

You will be assigned one of two roles: project manager for Mazierski, or sales manager for Kumar. You will try to negotiate a favourable contract for your employer. Read your specific instructions and act accordingly.

Do not read the information for the role you have not been assigned until after the negotiation has been completed. At that point you may wish to see what was behind your negotiating partner's position.

Kumar Integration/Mazierski Software: Project Bidding

Mazierski Software Handout

Do not read this section unless you have been assigned this role or you have completed the simulation. Ignoring this direction will reduce your learning experience from participating in this exercise.

You are the project manager for Mazierski Software, a large systems integrator that has just been awarded a $100,000 fixed-price contact to develop a Customer Relationship Management software subsystem for an existing client. Your proposal anticipates 500 hours of development time at a standard billing rate of $180 and ongoing warranty for a year. If your work is late, you will have to pay a late fee of $5,000 for every week that the project is delayed past your committed end date.

On investigating, you find that your firm does not have sufficient staff to meet the contract's obligations. You only have 200 hours available, at a fully loaded cost of $85 per hour. Overtime hours are available at twice the fully loaded cost, but even if you use these, you will complete the project two weeks late.

An alternative to doing the project in-house would be to subcontract it to a smaller local firm, Kumar Integration. You don't know much about this firm, but you do know that they are likely to be less expensive than your own staff, that they have a reputation for doing good-quality work, and that they always complete projects on time. If you use them, however, your warranty costs for the following year will increase by $10,000.

Required

Your job as project manager is to negotiate a favourable contract with the subcontractor, Kumar.

Summary of Costs	Do In-House	Subcontract

Negotiation	Contactor Offer	Subcontractor Bid

Kumar Integration/Mazierski Software: Project Bidding

Kumar Integration Handout

Do not read this section unless you have been assigned this role or you have completed the simulation. Ignoring this direction will reduce your learning experience from participating in this exercise.

You are the sales manager for a small local systems integrator, Kumar Integration, which has just lost a bid for a contract to develop a Customer Relationship Management software subsystem for a new client. Your proposal included 550 hours of development time at a standard billing rate of $150 as well as ongoing free warranty for a year. The client has told you that the bid was won by a larger firm, Mazierski Software, which already does a lot of work for it.

Soon after losing the bid, Mazierski's project manager calls you to find out whether you would like to subcontract the entire project, as it does not have all the resources it needs to complete the job. It could complete the job itself, but it wants to look into the option of subcontracting.

On review, you establish that your firm has excess resources that could immediately be applied to the project, and that you could finish the work on time. You have 800 available hours at a fully loaded cost of $65 per hour. Warranty for the year would cost about $5,000.

Required

Your job as sales manager is to negotiate a favourable contract with Mazierski.

Summary of Costs	Do In-House	Subcontract

Negotiation	Contactor Offer	Subcontractor Bid

HORVATH CHEMICALS: ACTIVITY-BASED BUDGETING

Charles Plant

This simulation has two parts. In Part A, the class will be broken into groups. You will take one of two roles: Vice President of Sales, or CFO of Horvath. Read your specific instructions and negotiate a revenue budget and a sales expense budget. In Part B, you will be given more information; then your group will be required to develop a budget using activity-based budgeting techniques.

PART A

Horvath Chemicals supplies other companies with chemical products. For the past three years, total revenues and sales expenditures have been as follows:

Year	Actual revenue	Sales expenditure
2003	$ 116,789,000	$ 5,840,000
2004	124,852,000	6,867,000
2005 – Estimated	136,471,000	8,188,000

The company is constructing its budget for 2006. In this process, the CFO and the VP Sales contribute unique information and have their own interests in the outcome.

Horvath Chemicals: Activity-Based Budgeting

I — Chief Financial Officer Handout

Do not read this section unless you have been assigned this role or you have completed the simulation. Ignoring this direction will reduce your learning experience from participating in this exercise.

You are the CFO of Horvath Chemicals. You are currently planning the 2006 budget with the VP Sales. It looks like 2006 will be another good year, but you have no information yet on just how good the year will be. You need to find out from the VP Sales what amounts he thinks should be budgeted for revenues and sales expenditures.

Your compensation plan, which cannot be changed, pays you a bonus based on profit. While there are other expenses that contribute to profit, in the sales department, profit is determined by subtracting sales costs from revenues. Thus, your objective is to maximize the profit contribution from this department by maximizing revenue and minimizing the sales expenditure.

Required

Negotiate the 2006 budgets for revenue and sales expenses.

Group name

Revenue budget

Sales expense budget

Horvath Chemicals: Activity-Based Budgeting

II — Vice President of Sales Handout

Do not read this section unless you have been assigned this role or you have completed the simulation. Ignoring this direction will reduce your learning experience from participating in this exercise.

You are the VP of Sales of Horvath Chemicals. You are currently planning the 2006 budget with the CFO. It looks like 2006 will be another good year; your analysis shows that revenues could increase to $150 million as long as the sales budget exceeds $8.7 million. To play it safe, however, a sales budget of $9.2 million would virtually guarantee revenues above $150 million.

The CFO is not aware of any of your projections; this is why she is looking for your plan for 2006. She wants to know what the company should budget for revenue in the year and how much you will need for sales spending.

Your compensation plan, which cannot be changed, pays you a bonus of $25,000 for meeting revenue targets that are set in the budget. You also get $5,000 for every $1 million that revenue exceeds that budget level.

Required

1. Negotiate the 2006 budgets for revenue and sales expenses.
2. Record your negotiation results with the following headings:

Group name

Revenue budget

Sales expense budget

PART B

Ignore the results achieved in Part A of this case when completing Part B. You will be asked for your results for Parts A and B at the end of this exercise.

After much analysis of past results as well as much debate about future expectations, the following breakdown of revenue for the past years as well as a budget for the next year has been agreed on.

Revenue	Actual 2003	Actual 2004	Estimated 2005	Budget 2006
Old clients/Old products	105,987,000	107,445,880	111,118,280	125,553,320
Old clients/New products	6,562,000	7,218,200	7,940,020	8,734,022
New clients	4,240,000	10,187,920	17,412,700	14,883,658
Total revenue	116,789,000	124,852,000	136,471,000	149,171,000

Further analysis has been performed on the activities, resources, and costs of the sales department. The following summarizes next year's activities and their planned impact.

- *Developing marketing materials.* The company has introduced the same number of products each year for the past three years, and it plans to introduce the same number of products in 2006.
- *Trade shows.* The company has attended the same five trade shows each year for the past few years and has no plan to change this.
- *Cold calling.* Analysis has determined that each hour of cold calling by sales people eventually results in $500 of revenue from new clients.
- *Account management.* Account management represents time spent with old clients on old products. Each hour of account management work is expected to produce $2,000 of revenue.
- *New product introduction.* This time is spent introducing new products to old clients. Every hour of this activity is expected to produce $1,000 of new-product revenue with old clients.
- *Obtaining new clients.* This activity involves taking the results of the cold calls and turning prospects into actual new customers. An hour of time in this activity is expected to produce $1,000 of revenue from new clients.
- *Management.* This is the time spent by the ten sales managers and the VP of Sales. There will be no need to add any staff in this area in 2006.
- *Administration.* Administration has been found to equal 10 percent of the time spent in the preceding seven activities.
- *Other.* This is a catchall for miscellaneous other activities. It has been running consistently at approximately 6,000 hours per year.

The resources used by these activities are as follows:

Hours	Actual 2003	Actual 2004	Estimated 2005	Budget 2006
Developing mktg material	3,600	3,600	3,600	
Trade shows	2,000	2,000	2,000	
Cold calling	8,480	20,376	34,825	
Account management	52,993	53,723	55,559	
New product introduction	6,562	7,218	7,940	
Obtaining new clients	4,240	10,188	17,413	
Management	22,000	22,000	22,000	
Administration	9,988	11,910	14,334	
Other	6,937	6,325	6,089	
Total hours	116,800	137,340	163,760	
Dollars per hour	50	50	50	
Total expenditure	5,840,000	6,867,000	8,188,000	

Required

Use the chart shown above to figure out the total expenditure that will be required in 2006 to increase revenue from $136 million to $149 million.

1. Negotiate a new budget for 2006 based on the role you were assigned in Part A.
2. Discuss how the negotiation process differed between Parts A and B.

YORK WIRELESS

Charles Plant

PART A — Quality Analysis

York Wireless has been manufacturing cellular phones for several years. At present, it is experiencing a number of quality problems, which have been causing sales to decline. The future does not look good. The company is now looking for any possible ways to save money. One approach that has been introduced involves topping up managers' bonuses for any real cost savings generated. Similarly, managers whose costs increase above budgetary levels have their bonus reduced. This method for calculating bonuses cannot be changed this year.

York's customers determine cell phone quality in relation to three elements: sound quality, screen failure, and total unit collapse. The company has recently reviewed the total costs of quality for the Engineering and Assembly Departments and has found the following costs for the past year.

	Engineering		Assembly		
	Prevention	Appraisal	Internal failure	External failure	Total
Sound quality	50,000	70,000	400,000	400,000	920,000
Screen failure	20,000	30,000	300,000	350,000	700,000
Unit collapse	100,000	80,000	250,000	250,000	680,000
	170,000	180,000	950,000	1,000,000	2,300,000

In addition, the Marketing Department has researched the customer base and found that the degree of importance that customers place on each element of quality is as follows:

	Importance
Sound quality	60%
Screen failure	30
Unit collapse	10
	100%

Further research indicates that an overall increase in the total costs of prevention and appraisal ($350,000) of 20 percent would cause a 20 percent reduction in the total costs of internal and external failure ($1,950,000). This spending would probably improve the company's customer relations and cause sales to rebound.

The assembly manager, who is responsible for the costs of internal and external failure, is especially keen to reduce costs. But to do this, the engineering manager who is responsible for prevention and failure will have to increase costs.

Required

In groups, take on either the job of the engineering manager or the job of the assembly manager.

1. First of all, use the following chart to calculate how much should be spent in total in each area.

	Total	Quality cost %	Importance	Value index	Required spending
Sound quality	920,000		60%		
Screen failure	700,000		30		
Unit collapse	680,000		10		
	2,300,000		100%		

2. Calculate how much should be spent in each area in order to improve the company's quality.

	Engineering		Assembly		
	Prevention	Appraisal	Internal failure	External failure	Total
Sound quality					
Screen failure					
Unit collapse					

3. Negotiate an equitable solution to the cost reduction problem between the two managers.

PART B — Value Chain Analysis

Rizzo Telephones is a large Canadian specialty retail chain that sells only telephones and telephony products to consumer markets. The highest selling and most profitable product is the Petrilli Cordless Phone, which is sold for $100. A Wal-Mart store has opened nearby and is selling the identical phone for $90. Rizzo currently buys these phones from a Canadian distributor called Colavecchia Distribution. Rizzo has asked to meet with Colavecchia and Petrilli Telecom to discuss the Wal-Mart competition and how Rizzo can reduce its costs to remain competitive with Wal-Mart.

Take one of the three roles for this simulation. Read your specific instructions in order to reduce the market price.

Handout — Rizzo Telephones

Do not read this section unless you have been assigned this role or you have completed the simulation. Ignoring this direction will reduce your learning experience from participating in this exercise.

You are a large Canadian specialty retail chain that sells only telephones and telephony products to consumer markets. Your highest selling and most profitable product is the Petrilli Cordless Phone, which you sell for $100. A Wal-Mart store has opened nearby and is selling the identical phone for $90. Your store has a lot more choice and better service, but you need to match Wal-Mart's price and get your price down to $90 per phone to remain competitive in the market.

You currently buy these phones from a Canadian distributor called Colavecchia Distribution, which sells the phones to you for $75, which includes shipping to your warehouse. You buy the phones and have them shipped to your central warehouse; your warehouse then ships them to stores as needed. Your warehouse costs and your costs of shipping to stores total $6 per phone. Your costs per phone to operate your stores have been determined through activity-based costing to be $9.

You have been approached by another distributor who operates internationally. This distributor will sell you the phones at a price of $66 to your warehouse or $70 to your stores directly. You could also buy the phones directly from Petrilli, but Petrilli could only ship to your warehouse. You have these choices:

1. Continue to buy in the same way and at the same price, and simply reduce your price to $90.
2. Buy from the new distributor for $66 and have it shipped to your warehouse. You would still face costs of $6 per phone for internal shipping and warehousing as well as $9 per phone for retail operating costs.
3. Buy from the new distributor for $70 and have it shipped directly to your stores. You would then still have $9 per phone retail operating costs.
4. Making a new deal with Colavecchia by getting it to reduce its price to you.
5. Buy the phones directly from Petrilli at a price to be negotiated. Petrilli would ship the phones directly to your warehouse.

You have called a meeting with Colavecchia and Petrilli to get their proposals.

Handout — Petrilli Telecom

Do not read this section unless you have been assigned this role or you have completed the simulation. Ignoring this direction will reduce your learning experience from participating in this exercise.

Petrilli, your employer, is a large telephone manufacturer that sells directly to large retailers and through distributors to smaller retailers. One of your most respected products is the Petrilli Cordless Phone. You are currently selling these phones to many retailers. You sell them directly to Wal-Mart and through one of your distributors, Colavecchia Distribution, to Rizzo, a large Canadian retail chain. You are aware that Wal-Mart is retailing the phones for $90 and that this price is hurting Rizzo's business, as Rizzo sells the same phone for $100.

You currently manufacture these phones at a cost of $25. When you sell to distributors, the cost to you is $15 per phone for warehousing, shipping, and all transaction costs. When you sell directly to retailers, you can only ship to their warehouses, not to their stores. Because of economies of scale, it costs $20 per phone for warehousing, shipping, and all transaction costs when sales are made directly to retailers. Currently, you sell the phones to Colavecchia Distribution and all other distributors at a price of $50 per phone. Your price per phone when you sell directly to retailers varies between $55 and $65.

Rizzo has asked you for a meeting to discuss the competition from Wal-Mart and how you (i.e., Petrilli) could reduce its (i.e., Rizzo's) costs to remain competitive with Wal-Mart. Your choices are as follows:

1. Continue to sell in the same way through Colavecchia and at the same price.
2. Continue to sell in the same way through Colavecchia at a new price.
3. Encourage Rizzo to buy from another distributor. You would still sell the phones to this new distributor at a price of $50.
4. Sell directly to Rizzo at a price to be negotiated between $55 and $65 per phone.

Handout — Colavecchia Distribution

Do not read this section unless you have been assigned this role or you have completed the simulation. Ignoring this direction will reduce your learning experience from participating in this exercise.

Colavecchia, your employer, is a large Canadian specialty distributor that sells a variety of products to retailers, including telephones. One of your best retail clients is Rizzo Telephones. One of the phones you sell to Rizzo is the Petrilli Cordless Phone. You currently buy these phones from Petrilli, which sells the phones to you for $50. Through activity-based costing, you have determined that your costs per phone to operate your warehouses and ship to retailers are $8. You currently ship to Rizzo's central warehouse; if you shipped directly to the stores, your shipping and transaction costs would increase by $7 per phone. You currently sell the phones to Rizzo for $75.

You are aware that Wal-Mart is becoming a stronger competitor to Rizzo and that Rizzo is facing price pressure. You have visited the nearest Wal-Mart and found that it is retailing the phones at $90.

Rizzo has asked to meet with you and Petrilli Telecom to discuss the Wal-Mart competition and how Rizzo might reduce its costs to remain competitive with Wal-Mart.

FARRELL LIGHTING: ACTIVITY-BASED BUDGETING

Charles Plant

Farrell Lighting is Canada's largest firm of industrial lighting product assemblers for manufacturers. Farrell has had an interesting few years, with increases in revenues and decreases in profits, culminating in a decline of profits again in 2005. Revenues for 2003, 2004, and 2005 are summarized below. The year end is October 31 of each year.

Revenue	Actual 2003	Actual 2004	Estimated 2005
Product A	15,987,000	15,507,390	14,732,021
Product B	6,562,000	8,202,500	9,843,000
Product C	12,785,000	13,040,700	13,562,328
Product D	7,654,000	9,261,340	12,410,196
Product E	0	3,497,000	6,294,600
Total revenue	42,988,000	49,508,930	56,842,145

The company is now preparing its budget for the 2006 fiscal year. The president has approached her senior managers and asked them to prepare a budget for the upcoming year. The senior management team consists of the VP Sales, the VP Operations, and the VP Manufacturing. Each of these people is paid a bonus that is derived 50 percent from the level of profit and 50 percent from how their end-of-year results compare to budget. Thus a VP who is over budget in expenses will receive little or no bonus, while a VP who finishes a year on or below budget will earn a healthy bonus.

The costs incurred by each department over the last three fiscal years (including bonuses) are summarized below:

Expenses	Actual 2003	Actual 2004	Estimated 2005
Sales	8,426,347	10,397,359	12,500,671
Operations	8,421,401	9,406,377	10,445,251
Manufacturing	5,037,583	6,082,175	7,162,188
Administration	2,149,400	2,475,447	2,842,107
Total expenses	24,034,731	28,361,358	32,950,217

Further examination of Farrell's income statements shows that cost of goods sold before manufacturing expenses (thus not included in the numbers above) equals 40 percent of total revenue for all products in all years. This percentage is expected to stay the same in 2006. Administration is expected to remain at 5 percent of revenue in 2006. Data for expenses for each department have been assembled for each VP and have been sent separately to each VP.

The company's objective is to increase sales and profits in the year. Because the market is so flexible, sales on any product can be increased by a maximum of 20 percent or reduced by a maximum of 10 percent. The company cannot change the percentage of revenue for cost of goods sold or administration in 2006.

Required

There is both a group and an individual component to this case. Work in groups of three, with each member of the group assuming one of these: VP Sales, VP Operations, or VP Manufacturing. Information specific to each role is provided below. Do not read the information until you have been assigned a role; then read only the information for that role.

Your objective as a group is to prepare a budget for 2006 that will maximize the firm's profit and each VP's bonus. Each VP is expected to participate in negotiating the levels of revenue for each product. Using this revenue budget, negotiate a budget for each department's expenses for the year. It is up to each member of the group whether information about past expenditures is to be kept private or shared with all members of the group. You can choose to negotiate an expense budget with team members with or without reference to activity-based data. You can also choose whether or not you wish to share activity-based data among team members.

As a group:

(a) submit a budget for the firm that includes all revenue and expenses;
(b) explain the rationale for the sales budget you arrive at and for the expense budgets; *and*
(c) explain how the group arrived at its submission.

Farrell Lighting: VP Sales

Do not read this section unless you have been assigned this role or you have completed the simulation. Ignoring this direction will reduce your learning experience from participating in this exercise.

The activities in your department can be broken down into five areas: marketing, sales to agencies, direct sales, management, and administration. After much analysis of past results and debate about future expectations, the following breakdown of activities and how they relate to revenue for the past three years has been established. This chart indicates that every hour of work in marketing generates $5,000 of revenue in Product A.

Dollars of revenue per hour of work	Product A	Product B	Product C	Product D	Product E
Marketing	5,000	4,000	5,500	3,500	2,100
Sales to agencies	11,000	2,000	1,000	1,500	900
Direct sales	500	500	400	300	200

In addition, in each of the past three years the company has spent 12,000 hours on management and 15 percent of the total of marketing, sales to agencies, direct sales, and management on administration. The cost to the company in the Sales Department is $50 for each hour of work performed. This $50 amount included all salaries and overhead for the department.

You can use this information when negotiating a budget for expenses for your department; alternatively, you can ignore it.

The following individual assignments are to be included with your group's submission.

1. Acting individually, use the activity-based data to calculate the Sales Department's expected expenditures based on the revenue budget you have chosen.
2. Compare your department's ABB budget numbers to the amounts your group has budgeted, and explain any difference.
3. When preparing the budget, what behaviour did you notice among the group members?
4. Describe the culture of your group.

You should try to maximize the amount of the budget you negotiate in the group versus the amount awarded to other group members. Be prepared to provide calculations and explanations for individual work.

Farrell Lighting: VP Manufacturing

Do not read this section unless you have been assigned this role or you have completed the simulation. Ignoring this direction will reduce your learning experience from participating in this exercise.

The activities in your department can be broken down into five areas; purchasing, assembly, packaging, management, and administration. After much analysis of past results and debate about future expectations, the following breakdown of activities and their relationship to revenue for the past three years has been established. The table indicates that every hour of work in purchasing generates $3,100 of revenue in Product A.

Dollars of revenue per hour of work	Product A	Product B	Product C	Product D	Product E
Purchasing	3,100	1,500	5,100	4,400	4,900
Assembly	900	170	700	600	450
Packaging	1,600	500	10,500	2,500	1,000

In addition, in each of the past three years the company has spent 12,000 hours per year on management and 15 percent of the total of purchasing, assembly, packaging, and management on administration. The cost to the company in the Manufacturing Department is $32 for each hour of work performed. This $32 includes all salaries and overhead for the department.

You can use this information when negotiating a budget for expenses for your department; alternatively, you can ignore it.

The following individual assignments are to be included with your group's submission:

1. Acting individually, use the activity-based data to calculate the Manufacturing Department's expected expenditures, based on the revenue budget you have chosen.
2. Compare your department's ABB budget numbers to the amounts your group has budgeted, and explain any difference.
3. When preparing the budget, what behaviour did you notice among the group members?
4. Describe the culture of your group.

You should try to maximize the amount of the budget you negotiate in the group versus the amount awarded to other group members. Be prepared to provide calculations and explanations for individual work.

Farrell Lighting: VP Operations

Do not read this section unless you have been assigned this role or you have completed the simulation. Ignoring this direction will reduce your learning experience from participating in this exercise.

The activities in your department can be broken down into five areas: warehousing, shipping, returns, management, and administration. After much analysis of past results and debate about future expectations, the following breakdown of activities and their relationship to revenue for the past three years has been established. This chart shows that every hour of work in the Warehousing Department generates $1,900 of revenue in Product A.

Dollars of revenue per hour of work	Product A	Product B	Product C	Product D	Product E
Warehousing	1,900	45,000	4,400	5,200	3,300
Shipping	200	500	600	400	300
Returns	1,000	8,400	2,200	1,100	1,400

In addition, in each of the past three years, the company has spent 12,000 hours on management and 15 percent of the total of warehousing, shipping, returns, and management on administration. The cost to the company in the Operations Department is $40 for each hour of work performed. This $40 includes all salaries and overhead for the department.

You can use this information when negotiating a budget for expenses for your department; alternatively, you can ignore it.

The following individual assignments are to be included with your group's submission:

1. Acting individually, use the activity-based data to calculate the Operations Department's expected expenditures, based on the revenue budget you have chosen.
2. Compare your department's ABB budget numbers to the amounts your group has budgeted, and explain any difference.
3. When preparing the budget, what behaviour did you notice among the group members?
4. Describe the culture of your group.

You should try to maximize the amount of the budget you negotiate in the group versus the amount awarded to other group members. Be prepared to provide calculations and explanations for individual work.

CAR BUYER'S DILEMMA

Charles Plant

You will be assigned the role of either the buyer or the seller of a car. Analyze the options and negotiate with the other participants to reach an agreement. After you have all agreed on a course of action, each of you will be required to individually complete the following assignment. No group submission will be required on this simulation.

- *Seller.* The buyer will need to purchase a car to travel to a new job this summer. Your job is to find and sell him/her the perfect car.

  Find an advertised Honda Accord for between $15,000 and $25,000. Print off the ad to submit with your assignment. Gather the details from the ad relating to price, mileage, options, condition, and so on. You do not need to contact the real seller for this simulation.

  In one sitting, try to sell the car to the Buyer pair for the highest price you can negotiate. You can negotiate an upfront price, you can lend money to finance the purchase, or you can charge a rental amount or a lease. You must not tell the buyer the advertised price for the car. Try to obtain a price higher than the advertised price. You must reach an agreement.

- *Buyer.* You need to purchase a car to travel to a new job this summer. The seller will be trying to sell you a car.

  The seller will be approaching you with a used Honda Accord that carries a price of between $15,000 and $25,000. Do your research so that you know how much you should be paying for cars with a variety of years, options, and so on.

  In one sitting, you must negotiate and agree on a purchase price for the car. You should try to agree to a price lower than the advertised price, which you will not be told. You must reach an agreement.

Required

1. Using activity-based management techniques, describe the process you used to sell or buy the car.
2. Develop a capital budget for the purchase or sale of the car, using the sale price you negotiated.
3. Explain and discuss the technical, behavioural, and cultural attributes of activity-based management in relation to this exercise.
4. Explain and discuss the strategic implications of target costing as it relates to a firm's ability to compete with quality, cost, and time, and how it could have been used in this simulation to improve the ability to reach resolution on the price.

Your write-up should be in the style of a business report. It should use lots of headings, subheadings, and charts, and structured presentation, to make the information easy to read and understand.

TECHNORATION

Charles Plant

Technoration is a software company that produces a leading web-based customer relations management software application used by janitorial firms throughout the world. The Research and Development Department has three teams:

- Software development is done by a group of software engineers, who design, develop, and module-test the various modules that comprise the software suite that Technoration offers. The Software Development team is managed by the Manager of Software Development.
- Once the software engineers have completed their module testing, the software is turned over to a Software Testing team, which is managed by the Manager of Testing, whose team performs specialized system and user testing.
- The software is then released into production. When users have problems with the software, they contact the Software Support Team, which is managed by the Manager of Software Support. This team's job is to manage customer complaints, attempt to find the problems, and implement solution to the problems.

As of the end of 2005, sales growth has been excellent and the firm has been experiencing good profit increases. The company is planning to go public just after releasing its 2006 financial statements, so it is important to reduce costs during 2006 in order to maximize profits. In doing so, the company will be maximizing the selling price of its stock. All three managers have options in the company, which they can cash in the day the company goes public. Obviously, then, they are very interested in having a high market value.

An increase in profits in 2006 will mean that each manager's options will be worth $150,000. With profits in 2006 equal to those of 2005, the options will be worth $100,000. With any decline in profits in 2006, the options will be worth nothing. If the managers exercise the options when the company goes public with the 2006 results, those options will be extinguished and they will not be able to exercise them in 2007.

It will be harder to predict the value of options if they are still held at the end of 2007, as the value will depend somewhat on the performance of the stock market as a whole. At the end of 2007, if the managers still own options, it is likely that they will be worth $350,000 if 2007 profit is above that of 2005. If 2007 profits are the same as 2005, the options will likely be worth $200,000. If profit declines in 2007 versus 2005, the options will likely be worthless.

Each of the three managers also has a bonus plan. Any manager whose costs go down from 2005 to 2006 will earn a special bonus of $100,000. Any manager whose costs increase or stay the same in 2006 as in 2005 will get no bonus whatsoever. Managers cannot elect to pool bonuses or share them in any way.

The company has enjoyed strong 2005 and is planning its budget for 2006. The budget choices for the Research and Development Department are as follows:

- The company can reduce the time spent on software development by spending less time on design and module testing with the Software Development team. This will have no affect on sales in 2006 but will increase the costs for the Software Testing and Software Support teams. A dollar saved in Software Development will increase Software Testing expenses by 50 cents and Software Support expenses by 50 cents. This will cause expenses for 2006 to stay the same as in 2005; thus profits will remain constant. In 2007, however, under this option, sales are likely to grow and profits be the same as in 2005.

- The company can spend less on software testing in 2006 by shifting the testing to the Software Development team. This will increase profits, as a dollar saved in testing will increase development costs by 50 cents and will not change Software Support costs. In 2007, however, this action will cause sales to decline by 5 percent, and the company will have lower profits in 2007 than in 2005.
- The company can move to a "six sigma" level of quality by spending more on software development and software testing. This action would decrease support costs in 2006, but overall costs would be up. A one-dollar increase in development and testing would cause a 50-cent decline in support costs. In 2006 there would be no impact on sales, but profits would decline. But in 2007, sales would increase strongly and thereby increase profits over 2005 levels. It would probably also set up the company for an excellent few years after 2007.

Required

You will be assigned one of the following roles: Manager of Software Development, Manager of Software Testing, or Manager of Software Support. Analyze the options and negotiate with the other participants to reach an agreement on the course of action the firm should take in 2006. After you have all agreed on a course of action, each of you must individually complete the following assignment. No group submission will be required on this simulation.

1. Describe and explain:
   (a) the analysis done in preparation for the negotiation with other department managers, including both quantitative and qualitative factors;
   (b) the process used to reach a decision by the group;
   (c) the decision reached;
   (d) the reasons for that decision; *and*
   (e) the impact the decision will have on the company.

2. Explain and discuss the strategic implications of quality costing as it relates to a firm's ability to compete with quality, cost, and time.
3. Explain and discuss the technical, behavioural, and cultural attributes of quality costing, using examples experienced in your negotiation session.

Your write-up should be in the style of a business report. It should use lots of headings, subheadings, and charts, as well as a structured presentation to make the information easy to read and understand.

REORGANIZING HOSPITAL SERVICES

Alan J. Richardson

In 1997 the Ontario Ministry of Health, through the province's Health Services Restructuring Commission, decided to reorganize certain health services in order to achieve better operational efficiency and shorter wait times. In particular, in some communities with multiple health facilities, the ministry encouraged facilities to specialize in certain types of treatment in order to create Centres of Excellence (i.e., all of the specialists in a field would be in the same unit). This would allow more training opportunities and the development of best practices, as well as economies of scale (i.e., by operating at a higher volume at one location, specialized equipment could be used and procedures could be done more efficiently). This change required operations to be shifted from one facility to another. This was to be done with no additional costs to the taxpayer, which meant that any two units involved in a transfer of services were required to negotiate how much of the ministry's grant should be transferred from one unit to the other along with the services being transferred.

Waterloo General Hospital was the largest health care facility in the Kitchener-Waterloo area.[4] Also located in the Kitchener-Waterloo area was the smaller Kitchener Trauma Centre. A study of these two facilities by the Restructuring Commission recommended that all non-emergency orthopedic surgery (treatment of problems of the skeleton and musculature) be combined in the Kitchener Trauma Centre. This change would establish a team of five orthopedic surgeons at one location and allow for up-to-date technologies to be added to that facility. It was anticipated that this new centre would add new services to the area's health care network and would develop skills that would reduce the cost of performing individual surgeries while decreasing wait times for high-demand services such as hip and knee joint replacement surgery.

The financial impacts of this recommendation are summarized below. This information was available to both parties prior to the negotiations.

Financial Impact on Waterloo General Hospital

Cost component	Effect of reorganization	Cost saving per year	Comments
Physicians	Two orthopedic surgeons removed from staff	$450,000	
Nurses	Six orthopedic nurses removed from staff	$420,000	
Supplies	Supplies related to orthopedic surgery no longer ordered	$210,000	
Equipment	Specialized equipment (somewhat dated) sold for salvage value	$85,000	
Operating rooms	Operating rooms reassigned to other specialties but currently not needed to meet demand	$0	
Total cost savings		$1,165,000	

---

[4] This case is based on real circumstances but the location, names, and details have been changed.

Financial Impact on Kitchener Trauma Centre

Cost component	Effect of reorganization	Cost increase per year	Comments
Physicians	Two orthopedic surgeons added to staff	$450,000	There will also
Nurses	Six orthopedic nurses added to staff	$420,000	be a one-time cost of $20,000 to compensate the physicians and nurses for the relocation
Supplies	Supplies related to orthopedic surgery ordered	$210,000	
Equipment	Specialized equipment purchased (amortized cost shown)	$380,000	
Operating rooms	Operating rooms built to accommodate orthopedic surgery (amortized value shown)	$400,000	
Total cost increase		$1,860,000	$1,880,000

Required

You will be assigned the role of either CEO of Waterloo General Hospital or CEO of Kitchener Trauma Centre. Prepare your case for how much of the government grant you will give up/claim when implementing the reorganization. Negotiate with your counterpart and come to an agreement on a joint recommendation to the Ministry of Health on how the grant should be reallocated. Your instructor will collect the results of each set of negotiations and discuss the outcomes.

Identify which costs create the greatest difficulty in this negotiation and why the costs avoided and the costs incurred are not the same. Ignoring the directions provided by the Ontario government for how the reorganization is to be handled, can you suggest alternative ways to handle the financing of the reorganization?